TALKING ABOUT DEVELOPMENTAL PSYCHOLOGY

PROGRAM IN DEVELOPMENTAL PSYCHOLOGY AT THE UNIVERSITY OF NORTH CAROLINA AT CHAPEL HILL

KENDALL/HUNT PUBLISHING COMPANY
4050 Westmark Drive   Dubuque, Iowa 52002

Cover image © 2002 PhotoDisc, Inc.

Copyright © 2002 by the Department of Psychology at the University of North Carolina at Chapel Hill

ISBN 0-7872-9548-5

Kendall/Hunt Publishing Company has the exclusive rights to reproduce this work,
to prepare derivative works from this work, to publicly distribute this work,
to publicly perform this work and to publicly display this work.

All rights reserved. No part of this publication may be reproduced,
stored in a retrieval system, or transmitted, in any form or by any
means, electronic, mechanical, photocopying, recording, or otherwise,
without the prior written permission of Kendall/Hunt Publishing Company.

Printed in the United States of America

10 9 8 7 6 5 4 3 2 1

Contents

MODULE 1	IMPLICIT THEORIES OF CHILD DEVELOPMENT	1
MODULE 2	CAREERS IN CHILD DEVELOPMENT	3
MODULE 3	RESEARCH METHODS	9
MODULE 4	GENE-ENVIRONMENT INTERACTIONS	13
MODULE 5	IN VITRO FERTILIZATION	19
MODULE 6	INFLUENCES ON PRENATAL DEVELOPMENT	21
MODULE 7	THE MOZART EFFECT	23
MODULE 8	COG—THE HUMANOID ROBOT	35
MODULE 9	DESIGNING A BABY TOY	39
MODULE 10	BEHAVIORAL INHIBITION	41
MODULE 11	ATTACHMENT THEORY AS EXPLAINED BY ITS AUTHORS	51
MODULE 12	HARRY HARLOW'S EXPERIMENTS ON THE AFFECTIONAL RESPONSES OF THE YOUNG INFANT	65
MODULE 13	GENIE AND LANGUAGE ACQUISITION	79
MODULE 14	LANGUAGE DEVELOPMENT	87
MODULE 15	DEVELOPMENTALLY APPROPRIATE CHILDREN'S LITERATURE AND FILM	91
MODULE 16	CHILDREN AS EYEWITNESSES	95
MODULE 17	SOCIOMETRY AND SOCIAL NETWORKING	101
MODULE 18	SEX DIFFERENCES	107
MODULE 19	GENDER STEREOTYPES IN TEEN MAGAZINES	121
MODULE 20	MORAL DEVELOPMENT	123
MODULE 21	TELEVISION VIOLENCE AND AGGRESSION	129
MODULE 22	SELECTIVE BREEDING FOR HIGH AND LOW AGGRESSION	131
MODULE 23	JUVENILE DELINQUENCY	137

MODULE 24	BREUER AND THE CASE OF ANNA O.	141
MODULE 25	AUTISM AND MINDBLINDNESS	145
MODULE 26	RISK AND PROTECTIVE FACTORS IN DEVELOPMENT: A FILM ANALYSIS	154

PREFACE

Undergraduates enroll in courses on child development for various reasons. For some students, training in child development is a step toward a child-oriented career in developmental psychology, health, education, social work, etc. For other students, training in child development provides preparation for effective parenting. Still other students find child development to be an intrinsically interesting topic, worthy of study independent of any practical considerations. Given a topic that is compelling from so many perspectives, child development courses should be exciting intellectual adventures. Unfortunately, this is not always the case. Several excuses come to mind. Some are related to the problem that a century of research on children has led to a vast array of findings. Textbooks grow in length, and instructors face the challenge of packing more and more material into one semester. Related, even the most scholarly instructor has deep familiarity with only a small subset of the relevant topics. Another problem stems from the popularity of the topic: Child Development courses are almost always filled to capacity, which pressures universities toward larger and larger class sizes. Because of these constraints, and despite our best intentions, child development courses can become fast-paced, shallow monologues that bore even the most intelligent and motivated students.

What can be done about this? One solution is to provide students with opportunities to engage in the material, use it, and experience some degree of ownership. The modules in this book are designed to facilitate this interactive experience. We have made use of various formats that have proven effective in our own courses in child development. Some modules provide a relevant empirical article, a media report, or another original source and a set of discussion questions to get the ball rolling. Other modules provide a scenario or data set to seed conversation on a particular topic. Some modules build on a common experience (e.g., answering the questions on a temperament interview) as the basis for a conversation about development. Finally, some modules are designed to evoke student opinions or folk theories that are relevant to the study of child development.

We see many alternatives for how these modules can be used. In some class formats, the modules can form the basis for discussion groups that are separate from a main lecture (either in actual groups or in a chat-room format). In smaller sections, the modules can be used as auxiliary material during class or as homework. It is unlikely that any instructor will use all of the modules in a single semester, although they do cover the range of material that one finds in a traditional child development course. Note that the modules are not geared for use with any particular text.

We certainly hope that you will enjoy our book and that it will be a useful component of your training in child development. If you have any comments or suggestions about the modules or ideas for additional modules, please send us e-mail: Developmental_Psychology@unc.edu

MODULE 1

IMPLICIT THEORIES OF CHILD DEVELOPMENT

In this module, you will consider several questions designed to probe your implicit theories of child development and the concept of development in general.

INTRODUCTION

Several definitions of the term *development* have been offered over the years. How scientists define this term naturally depends on which factors they believe are necessary and sufficient to bring about changes in the individual. For example, one may consider development as involving the gradual unfolding of innate potentials. The implicit theory contained in this definition is that offspring inherit genetic programs from their parents that dictate the growth process and determine how the individual matures. Development may also be defined as the acquisition of new characteristics. Here the implicit theory is that learning and experiences direct the acquisition of new behaviors or other adaptive traits. Another definition states that development involves continuous interactions between biology and experiences. From this perspective, the very same experiences would be expected to produce different outcomes for different individuals because their effects are modulated by differences in genetic background. Taken together, these definitions and their implicit theories may remind you of the nature versus nurture debate that divided developmental theorists for many years.

In a course in child development, you encounter several theories that may remind you of the nature-nurture debate. Scientists use theories to organize information relevant to particular questions, generate testable hypothesis, and make predictions. You may not realize it, but you probably have your own theories of development, based on your experiences with the world. One useful starting point as you begin your study of child development is to focus on your own assumptions about development. This process will allow you to compare your definitions and the developmental processes they emphasize to those theories held by your classmates and to the theories you will encounter in your readings during the semester. The diversity of opinions you will see can make you aware of the aspects of your theory that might be arbitrary (if not wrong!) and suggest general definitions of development that capture both its descriptive and process aspects.

PART 1
Discussion Questions

1. Think of an acquaintance that has changed the most since you were both children. In what ways is that person different? When did this person change?
2. To what extent was the person an active cause of the changes you observed? Did external events also play a role?
3. Did the person you have in mind change suddenly or gradually?
4. Does this change affect the person in all contexts or only in specific situations (e.g., at school)?
5. Was this change specific to the person's culture or of a more universal nature?
6. Which of the following processes, alone or in combination, best accounts for changes you described in your answers to the preceding questions?
    a. the unfolding of a genetic program
    b. behavior modification through reward and punishment (i.e., social learning)
    c. socialization of personality, values, and behaviors
    d. natural transition across life-stages (e.g., onset of puberty)
    e. the result of a socially-prescribed transition (e.g., to kindergarten, to middle school, or to parenting)
    f. an interaction between person characteristics and those of the environment
    g. none of the above (you offer your own definition)

Selected Readings

Goldhaber, D. E. (2000). *Theories of Human Development: Integrative Perspectives.* Mayfield Publishing Company: Mountain View, CA.

James-Roberts, I. (2001). *Theories of child development: The epigenetic framework.* [On-line]. Available: http://k1.ioe.ac.uk/cdl/newSite/msccdev/pdfs/Epigenetics2001.pdf

Lerner, R. M. (2002). *Concepts and theories of human development* (3rd ed.). Laurence Earlbaum Associates: Mahweh, NJ.

Murray, T. R. (2000). *Comparing theories of child development.* Belmont, CA: Wadsworth.

MODULE 2

CAREERS IN CHILD DEVELOPMENT

From college professor to clinical psychologist to day-care supervisor, the field of child development offers ample opportunities to those with backgrounds in psychology. Advanced degrees are required for some careers in child development, but others do not require additional years of education. This module is designed to provide a context in which to assess your own interests in such careers. You will read about the various career options currently available for people with undergraduate and graduate degrees in developmental psychology.

INTRODUCTION

An accumulating body of research during the last decades has brought to the forefront a number of factors that can, for better or for worse, affect the development of our children. The most salient of these include physical health, parenting and the family environment, educational resources during the preschool years and school preparedness, as well as a number of psychological factors like attention and learning capacities and mental health. In the context of a growing awareness that the provision of adequate care and timely preventive measures across these different domains can make a significant difference for both the developing individual and for society, the number of career opportunities in child development has grown steadily in the last few decades.

PART 1
CAREERS IN CHILD DEVELOPMENT

The Table following is from Santrock (2001) and provides an extensive list of the kinds of careers in child development one may contemplate, along with their respective degree requirements and a description of the work entailed. This table is reproduced from the following source:

Jobs and Careers in Child Development and Related Fields

Jobs/careers	Degree	Education required
Child clinical psychologist or counseling psychologist	Ph.D. or Psy.D.	5–7 postundergraduate
Child life specialist	Undergraduate degree	4 years of undergraduate study
Child psychiatrist	M.D.	7–9 years postundergraduate
Child welfare worker	Undergraduate degree (minimum)	4 years minimum
College/university professor in child development, education, family development, nursing, social work	Ph.D. or master's degree	5–6 years for Ph.D. (or D.Ed.) postundergraduate; 2 years for master's degree postundergraduate
Day-care supervisor	Varies by state	Varies by state
Early childhood educator	Undergraduate degree (minimum)	4 years (minimum)
Elementary or secondary school teacher	Undergraduate degree (minimum)	4 years
Exceptional children teacher (special education teacher)	Undergraduate degree (minimum)	4 years or more (some states require a master's degree or passing a standardized exam to obtain a license to work with exceptional children).
Guidance counselor	Undergraduate degree (minimum); many have master's degree	4 years undergraduate; 2 years graduate
Pediatrician	M.D.	7–9 years medical school
Pediatric nurse	R.N.	2–5 years
Preschool/kindergarten teacher	Usually graduate degree	4 years
Psychiatric nurse	R.N.	2–5 years
School psychologist	Master's degree or Ph.D.	5–6 years of graduate work for Ph.D. or D.Ed.; 2 years for master's degree

Nature of training

Includes both clinical and research training: involves a 1-year internship in a psychiatric hospital or mental health facility.

Many child life specialists have been trained in child development or education but undergo additional training in child life programs that includes parent education, developmental assessment, and supervised work with children and parents.

Four years of medical school, plus an internship and residency in child psychiatry are required.

Coursework and training in social work or human services.

Take graduate courses, learn how to conduct research, attend and present papers at professional meetings.

The Department of Public Welfare in many states publishes a booklet with the requirements for a day-care supervisor.

Coursework in early childhood education and practice in day-care or early childhood centers with supervised training.

Wide range of courses, with a major or concentration in education.

Coursework in education, with a concentration in special education.

Coursework in education and counseling in a school of education; counselor training experience.

Four years of medical school, plus an internship and residency in pediatrics.

Courses in biological sciences, nursing care, and pediatrics (often in a school of nursing); supervised clinical experiences in medical settings.

Coursework in education with a specialization in early childhood education; state certification usually required.

Courses in biological sciences, nursing care, and mental health in a school of nursing; supervised clinical training in child psychiatric settings.

Includes coursework and supervised training in school settings, usually in a department of educational psychology.

Description of work

Child clinical psychologists or counseling psychologists diagnose children's problems and disorders, administer psychological tests, and conduct psychotherapy sessions. Some work at colleges and universities, where they do any combination of teaching, therapy, and research.

Child life specialists are employed by hospitals and work with children and their families before and after the children are admitted to the hospital. They often develop and monitor developmentally appropriate activities for child patients. They also help children adapt to their medical experiences and their stay at the hospital. Child life specialists coordinate their efforts with physicians and nurses.

The role of the child psychiatrist is similar to that of the child clinical psychologist, but the psychiatrist can conduct biomedical therapy (for example, using drugs to treat clients); the child clinical or counseling psychologist cannot.

Child welfare workers are employed by the Child Protective Services Unit of each state to protect children's rights. They especially monitor cases of child maltreatment and abuse and make decisions about what needs to be done to help protect the abused child from further harm and to help the child cope with prior abuse.

College and university professors teach courses in child development, family development, education, or nursing; conduct research; present papers at professional meetings; write and publish articles and books; and train undergraduate and graduate students for careers in these fields.

Day-care supervisors direct day-care or preschool programs, being responsible for the operation of the center. They often make decisions about the nature of the center's curriculum, may teach in the center themselves, work with and consult with parents, and conduct workshops for the staff or parents.

Early childhood educators usually teach in community colleges that award associate or bachelor's degrees in early childhood education with specialization in day care. They train individuals for careers in the field of day care.

Elementary and secondary teachers teach one or more subjects; prepare the curriculum; give tests, assign grades, and monitor students' progress; interact with parents and school administrators; attend lectures and workshops involving curriculum planning or help on special issues; and direct extracurricular programs.

Exceptional children teachers (also called special education teachers) work with children who are educationally handicapped (those who are mentally retarded, have a physical handicap, have a learning disability, or have a behavioral disorder) or who are gifted. They develop special curricula for the exceptional children and help them adapt to their exceptional circumstances. Special education teachers work with other school personnel and with parents to improve the adjustment of exceptional children.

The majority of guidance counselors work with secondary school students, assisting them in educational and career planning. They often give students aptitude tests and evaluate their interests, as well as their abilities. Guidance counselors also see students who are having school-related problems, including emotional problems, referring them to other professionals, such as school psychologists or clinical psychologists, when necessary.

Pediatricians monitor infants' and children's health and treat their diseases. They advise parents about infant and child development and the appropriate ways to deal with children.

Pediatric nurses promote health in infants and children, working to prevent disease or injury, assisting children with handicaps or health problems so they can achieve optimal health, and treating children with health deviations. Some pediatric nurses specialize in certain areas (for example, the neonatal intensive care unit clinician cares exclusively for newborns; the new-parent educator helps the parents of newborns develop better parenting skills). Pediatric nurses work in a variety of medical settings.

Preschool teachers direct the activities of prekindergarten children, many of whom are 4-year-olds. They develop an appropriate curriculum for the age of the children that promotes their physical, cognitive, and social development in a positive atmosphere. The number of days per week and hours per day varies from one program to another. Kindergarten teachers work with young children who are between the age of preschool programs and the first year of elementary school; they primarily develop appropriate activities and curricula for 5-year-old children.

Psychiatric nurses promote the mental health of individuals; some specialize in helping children with mental health problems and work closely with child psychiatrists to improve these children's adjustment.

School psychologists evaluate and treat a wide range of normal and exceptional children who have school-related problems; work in a school system and see children from a number of schools; administer tests, interview and observe children, and consult with teachers, parents, and school administrators; and design programs to reduce the child's problem behavior.

Activity

After examining Table 1, select a career option that you find especially interesting. Then, locate a person who works in that profession and interview them. Ask for information about recent trends in that profession as well as that person's own experiences and recommendations for others who may want to pursue a career in that field. Interviewing someone currently working in your field of interest is a valuable way to learn about the profession.

PART 2
REQUIRED READING

The following article provides a detailed account of the demands currently placed on the professional psychologist. It also contains a useful discussion of the various factors that will define this profession in the years to come.

WHERE ARE NEW PSYCHOLOGISTS GOING?

APA's Research Office presents employment and salary data at the 2001 Annual Convention.

Reshma Ballie

From Monitor on Psychology, 11, December 2001 by R. Ballie. Copyright © 2001 by the American Psychological Association. Reprinted with permission.

What types of jobs are new doctorates going into? What kinds of skill sets do psychology majors have that make them marketable? How should recent grads market themselves to find jobs?

These were just some of the questions William Pate II, a research associate with APA's Research Office, answered at APA's 2001 Annual Convention in San Francisco. Pate presented data from surveys conducted by the APA Research Office, National Science Foundation and U.S. Department of Education to provide future psychologists with objective information on the job market, realistic expectations of debt and median starting salaries.

In an interview after convention, Pate answered the following key questions about the job market for psychologists.

Q. The Proportion of Psychologists Working in Academia Dropped from 55 Percent in 1973 to 33 Percent in 1999. What's Behind that Change?

Two changes occurred that contributed to this shift. First, the number of psychologists trained in the practice subfields increased during this period, while the number of those in academe remained relatively stable. This difference in growth created the percentage drop of psychologists in academe. It's not as though psychologists have been actively leaving academe in large numbers for the private sector.

The growth in the number of practicing psychologists was primarily fueled by changes in the laws governing who could and could not be reimbursed for treatment. The inclusion of psychologists opened up health service provision as an employment option. Responding to the perceived need, professional schools of psychology came into being in the early 1970s and their numbers have continued to grow, albeit more slowly in recent years.

A second reason for the drop in the proportion of psychologists in academe is that psychologists' skills have been increasingly recognized in the job market. This is especially the case in more nontraditional settings such as the business world and in government. Graduates have a strong basis in research methodology and analysis that allow them to apply themselves in a variety of occupations that require an understanding of how people behave in their environment, be it a police force, a computer interface or in the boardroom. Rather than being automatically stereotyped as a therapist, more and more psychologists are being seen as applied scientists.

Q. What Are Some of the Most Noticeable Demographic Shifts in the Field of Psychology?

The proportion of women among new psychology doctorates had increased from 33 percent in 1976 to 70 percent in 1999. Yet, women made up only 46 percent of psychology PhDs in the workforce in 1999.

Meanwhile, the proportion of minorities among new doctorates in psychology increased from 8 percent in 1977 to 15 percent in 1999, but only 9 percent of psychology PhDs in the workforce were minorities.

Q. Why Are Psychology Students Well-suited and Well-prepared for the Job Market?

Because they are trained to critically evaluate information and research. This ability to look at and evaluate data and information is a central tenet of psychology. This skill is learned and applied to the understanding of human behavior. Areas of application include personnel selection and training, developing user-friendly computer software, the delivery of psychological services to victims of natural and man-made disasters, the profiling of serial killers, the creation of effective commercials that increase the sale of a product, and so on.

As scientists, psychologists are well versed in the scientific method and statistical analysis. This allows one to design sound research that yields valid and reliable data, which can be applied to the solution of social problems, used to inform policy-makers, and determine new product lines. The ability to translate the results of basic research into tangible and relevant outcomes is an important skill. A person who can do this, and who can also communicate across a variety of audiences, is a valuable asset to any university, organization, or company.

Q. How Should Graduates Go about Job Hunting?

Make yourself stand out. In an increasingly competitive job market, you need to tailor your presentation to the desired position. This requires a close examination of your skills and experience and an ability to effectively communicate why you, among so many other applicants, should be chosen for the job.

If you don't get your dream job, be sure to find one that will provide you with opportunities to develop or refine your skills for the next one.

Discussion Questions

1. What are some reasons why recent doctorates in psychology are pursuing careers outside of colleges and universities?
2. Describe some of the work options available in child development for individuals with masters level degrees in Psychology.
3. What are some of the work options for those with bachelors degrees in child development?

4. Most research careers in child development require a Ph.D. degree. If this is your personal choice, how should you prepare for it? What are the requirements for admission in graduate programs in psychology? What does graduate training consist of? What do you need to accomplish as a graduate student to be a competitive candidate in the academic world?

MODULE 3

RESEARCH METHODS

In this module, you will explore a series of questions designed to help you consider some of the challenges that researchers face as they apply the scientific method to the study of developmental psychology.

■ INTRODUCTION

When designing a research project, psychologists work through a series of steps in order to collect reliable data that can be used to inform the scientific community about a particular developmental phenomenon. To familiarize yourself with these steps you will design a developmental study to address one of the following questions.

1. What factors account for the changes seen in mother-child conversations over time?
2. Are individuals who were physically punished in infancy and childhood more likely to become aggressive individuals as they develop?
3. Are there gender differences in children's play behaviors with peers?
4. What environmental factors are related to the development of memory strategies?
5. Can a specific diet and exercise program prevent obesity?
6. Are younger children more susceptible to the effects of divorce than older children?

PART 1
■ DESIGN YOUR STUDY

- Causes vs Relationships

Should an experiment be conducted or should a correlational study be completed? Consider the key differences between these two types of studies while specifying the aim of your research. Provide a rationale for your choice.

- Research Design

Are you designing a longitudinal or a cross-sectional study? What age-range do you plan to investigate? Discuss/outline the advantages and disadvantages of each type of design and determine which one is more appropriate to address your research question.

- Is your Question Amenable to research as Formulated?

Rewrite your research question taking into account the choices you made in steps 1 and 2.

- Selecting a Research Sample

What sample size do you need to insure the generalizability of your findings? What population of individuals will you sample from? Are gender, ethnicity, and age important variables to control for? What steps will you take to constitute a valid sample?

- Specifying the Variables

What variables do you need to measure in order to answer your research question? Do not turn this into an impossible task. Come up with a set of potential variables that may be of relevance to answer your research question. Then, identify the key 2-4 variables that you will need to measure to answer your research question. For each variable: name it, describe the procedure you will use to measure it, and label it as an independent or dependent variable.

- Measurement Issues

How do you measure (i.e., collect information about) each of your variables? What instrument(s) or data collection technique(s) do you plan to use to measure these variables? How will you make sure that your measures appropriately capture the information you need?

PART II
Discussion Questions

1. Consider adding the following values to the ages of your selected sample [6 months, 1 year, 5 years, 10 years]. How would these changes to the ages of your sample change your choice of methods to collect information?

2. What does the term "ecological validity" refer to? Is the project you designed ecologically valid? What aspects of your research study make you say so? What aspects would you change to make it more ecologically valid?

3. At what age do you think children are capable of providing informed consent to participate? Why? When working with young children what types of procedures should be in place to ensure that proper consent to participate is granted?

Suggested Readings

Applebaum, M. I., & McCall, R. B. (1983). Design and analysis in developmental psychology. In P. H. Musen (Ed.) *Handbook of child psychology.* Vol. 1. (4th ed., pp. 415–476). New York: Wiley.

Menard, S. (1991). Longitudinal research. *Series: Quantitative Applications in the Social Sciences, 76,* 3–80.

MODULE 4

GENE-ENVIRONMENT INTERACTIONS

In this module you will learn about how early environmental factors can alter the expression of a specific trait. Although there are numerous claims that the nature-nurture debate described by Galton at the end of the 19th century is now obsolete, several areas of research continue to operate under the assumption that phenotypic variability can be accounted for by genetic and environmental influences that act independently and additively. In research on humans, determining whether genes and environments act multiplicatively (i.e., through interactions, primarily) or additively (i.e., each brings a contribution independently of the other) has been a daunting task because the necessary experimental controls can not be implemented for obvious ethical reasons. In this module you will read an article in which the investigators, working with laboratory rats, were able to examine how genetic and environmental influences jointly act to produce phenotypic differences in intelligence.

INTRODUCTION

There are not many options for evaluating whether genes or environments are more important to the development of a given phenotype. A human study designed to thoroughly examine such a question would, at the very least require a 2×2 experimental design. That is, one would need to contrast four conditions involving two levels of genetic endowment and two levels of environment. Twin studies are widely used to evaluate the relative contribution of genes and environments. However, twin studies rest solely on mathematical techniques (i.e., shared and unshared variance between groups) because it is not possible to randomly assign genetic endowment groups to environmental treatment groups. Moreover, it is not clear whether the environments of twins reared apart really differ (because of strict adoption policies), or if they do, to what extent. Nor do we know what the effects of a shared prenatal environment may be.

PART 1
REQUIRED READING

The research conducted by Cooper & Zubek was designed to test for possible differential effects of enriched versus restricted early environments on the problem-solving ability of bright and dull rats. A *normal environment* condition was also added as a third condition. Note that this so-called normal environment consists of the standard conditions under which laboratory animals are normally kept. It is under these conditions that selective breeding for high and low problem-solving ability took place.

EFFECTS OF ENRICHED AND RESTRICTED EARLY ENVIRONMENTS ON THE LEARNING ABILITY OF BRIGHT AND DULL RATS[1]

R. M. Cooper and John P. Zubek

Copyright © 1958. Canadian Psychological Association. Reprinted with permission.

Several recent surveys of the literature (2, 3, 4, 9) reflect the increased emphasis being placed upon study of the relationship between early environment and later behaviour in animals. Learning ability has received particular attention, and several studies have shown that the learning ability of adult animals is affected by the quality of their infant environment. More specifically, they indicate that animals raised in "enriched" or "stimulating" environments are superior in adult learning ability to animals raised in "restricted" or "unstimulating" environments.

These results were obtained with animals possessing a *normal* heritage of learning ability; hence there remains the possibility of differential effects for animals of superior or inferior endowment. The present study was designed to explore this possibility. Its specific object was to test for possible differential effects of enriched and restricted early environments on the problem-solving ability of bright and of dull rats.

METHOD

Subjects

Forty-three rats of the McGill bright and dull strains (F_{13}) served as subjects. They were divided into 4 experimental groups: a bright-enriched group containing 12 rats (6 males, 6 females); a dull-enriched group containing 9 rats (4 males, 5 females); a bright-restricted group containing 13 rats (6 males, 7 females); and a dull-restricted group containing 9 rats (4 males, 5 females). Normally reared rats served as controls.

Environments

The 4 groups of experimental animals were placed in 4 cages which occupied a grey painted room 12' × 6' × 8'. At one end of the room a window allowed diffuse light to pass through. A large rectangular partition, suspended from the ceiling, divided the room lengthways. The two restricted cages were placed on one side of the partition, the two enriched cages on the other side. The side of the partition facing the restricted cages was grey, matching the colour of the room. The side of the partition facing the enriched cages was white with "modernistic" designs painted upon it in black and luminous paint. The partition was so placed that animals in the restricted environment were unable to see the enriched cages.

The 4 cages, each measuring 40" × 25" × 13", were covered with 1/2-inch wire mesh. Each of the enriched cages contained the following objects: ramps, mirrors, swings, polished balls, marbles, barriers, slides, tunnels, bells, teeter-totters, and springboards, in addition to food boxes and water pans. Some of the objects were painted black and white, and all were constructed so that they could

---

[1]This research was supported by a grant in aid from the Associate Committee on Applied Psychology of the National Research Council of Canada. The writers wish to acknowledge their indebtedness to Dr. D. O. Hebb for his critical reading of the manuscript.

easily be shifted to new positions in the cage. The restricted cages were identical with the enriched ones in size and mesh coverings, but contained only a food box and a water pan.

Test Apparatus

The 12 problems of the Hebb-Williams closed field maze were administered in the manner described by Rabinovitch and Rosvold (8).

Procedure

The 4 groups of animals were kept in their respective environments from the time of weaning at 25 days of age until the age of 65 days, when testing on the Hebb-Williams maze was begun. They were also kept there throughout the testing period.

Since one of the restricted and one of the enriched cages received more light than the others did from the window, the animals were shifted every three days to equate for this difference. In addition, the objects in each of the enriched cages were moved about at random every three or four days. During these moving periods and while the cages were being cleaned all animals were given the same amount of handling.

RESULTS

For purposes of statistical analysis and interpretation of the data the performances of the enriched and restricted animals were compared with the performances of 11 bright and 11 dull animals raised in a "normal" laboratory environment. These were the animals that formed two control groups in an experiment by Hughes and Zubek (6).

Effect of the Enriched Environment

In Table I are recorded the mean error scores for the bright-enriched group, the dull-enriched group, and the bright and dull animals raised in a normal environment. It can be seen that the average number of errors made by the bright animals in the enriched environment is only slightly below that of the bright animals raised under normal conditions (111.2 vs. 117.0). This difference is not statistically significant ($t = 0.715, p > .4$). On the other hand, the error scores of the dull animals raised in an enriched environment are considerably below those of dull animals reared in a normal environment (119.7 vs. 164.0). This difference of 44.3 errors is significant ($t = 2.52, p > .02 < .05$). The results indicate, therefore, that an enriched early environment can improve considerably the learning ability of dull animals, while having little or no effect on that of bright animals.

Effect of the Restricted Environment

Table II shows the mean error scores of the bright-restricted group, the dull-restricted group, and the bright and dull animals raised in a normal environment. It is seen that the bright-restricted group made many more errors than the normally raised bright animals. The difference of 52.7 errors is statistically significant ($t = 4.06, p < .001$). On the other hand there is no significant difference between the dull-restricted group and the normally raised dull animals ($t = 0.280, p > .7$). Thus the dull animals were not affected by their restricted early experience while the bright animals were significantly impaired in learning ability.

TABLE I

Mean Error Scores for Bright and Dull Animals Reared in Enriched and Normal Environments

	Enriched environment	Normal environment
Bright	111.2	117.0
Dull	119.7	164.0

TABLE II

Mean Error Scores for Bright and Dull Animals Reared in Restricted and Normal Environments

	Restricted environment	Normal environment
Bright	169.7	117.0
Dull	169.5	164.0

Comparative Effects of Enriched and Restricted Environments

Tables I and II also indicate the degree of improvement produced in the dull animals by their period of enriched experience, and the degree of retardation which the bright animals suffered because of their impoverished experience. Although the dull-enriched group averaged 8.5 more errors than did the bright-enriched, this difference is not significant ($t = .819, p > .5$). In other words, after undergoing a period of enriched experience the dull animals became equal in learning ability to the bright animals. The difference between the bright- and dull-restricted groups in Table II is also obviously insignificant; thus, the bright animals, after a period of early impoverished experience, showed no better learning ability than did the dull animals.

DISCUSSION

The results clearly show that both enriched and restricted early environments have differential effects on the learning abilities of bright and of dull rats. A period of early enriched experience produces little or no improvement in the learning ability of bright animals, whereas dull animals are so benefited by it that they become equal to bright animals. On the other hand, dull animals raised in a restricted environment suffer no deleterious effects, while bright animals are retarded to the level of the dulls in learning ability.

Although it had been anticipated that the two extremes of environment would have differential effects on the bright and dull animals, the bright-enriched animals were still expected to perform better than the dull-enriched animals. Bright animals, with their presumably better cerebral functioning, would be expected to make better use of the extra experience afforded by an enriched environment than would dull animals, with their presumably inferior cerebral functioning. The bright-enriched group did in fact make fewer errors, and the difference, though not statistically significant, suggests the possibility of a real difference in learning ability which the twelve problems of the Hebb-Williams test failed to reveal. The ceiling of the test may have been too low to differentiate the animals, that is, the problems may not have been sufficiently difficult to tax the ability of the bright rats. This has happened with tests of human intelligence such as the Stanford-Binet (1), on which adults of varying ability may achieve similar I.Q. scores although more difficult tests reveal clear differences between them. It might also be suggested that it is relatively more difficult for the bright animals to reduce their error scores, say from 120 to 100, than for the dull animals to reduce theirs from 160 to 140.

In spite of these possible qualifications of the present results for the enriched environment, it seems reasonable to accept them pending future experimentation.

The effects of the restricted environment are not so difficult to accept. Under such conditions the bright animals, even with their superior learning capacity, would be expected to show an inferior performance. Learning is a function of experience as well as of capacity, and hence, under conditions that severely limit experience, the superior capacity of the bright animals is never fully utilized and they perform far below their potential level. On the other hand, not much decrement would be expected in the dull animals, since they are already functioning at a low level of intellectual capacity.

What physiological mechanism or mechanisms underlie these changes in learning ability? Several theories have attempted to explain the relationship between sensory stimulation and learning behaviour, perhaps the most systematic being that of Hebb (5). Hebb has suggested that neural patterns or "cell assemblies," which he regards as the physiological basis of learned behaviour, are built up over a period of time through varied stimulation coming through specific sensory pathways. This stimulation is especially effective if it occurs during infancy. Others (7, 9) also believe that varied stimulation coming through non-specific projection pathways (e.g., the thalamic-reticular system) aids in the learning process by keeping the brain in an alert state. Thus at the neurophysiological level varied stimulation seems to play a dual role in the learning process; it may act directly on cerebral cells to form cell assemblies, and may also aid learning by keeping the brain "primed" or alert.

If, then, varied stimulation has such an important role in establishing the physiological components (e.g., cell assemblies) underlying learned behaviour, it seems reasonable to assume that a certain level of varied stimulation is necessary if learning (i.e., establishment of cell assemblies) is to occur with maximum efficiency. It may also be assumed that the initial difference in learning ability between the bright and dull rats in some way reflects an underlying neurophysiological difference in their capacity to "utilize" such stimulation. On the basis of these assumptions the present findings might be explained as follows.

In a *normal* environment the level of stimulation is sufficient to permit the building up of cell assemblies (or some other neurophysiological unit underlying learned behaviour) in the superior brains of the bright animals. It is not sufficient, however, to permit them to be readily built up in the inferior brains of the dull animals. In a *restricted* environment the level of stimulation is so low that it is inadequate for the building up of cell assemblies even with the superior cerebral apparatus of the bright rats, who therefore show a retardation in learning ability. The dulls, however, are not retarded further, since the level of stimulation provided by the normal environment was already below their threshold for the establishment of cell assemblies. In the *enriched* environment the level of stimulation is above the higher threshold of the dull animals, who consequently show improvement in learning ability. The brights show little or no improvement because the extra stimulation is largely superfluous, that provided by a normal environment being adequate for the building up of cell assemblies.

Such an interpretation is open to several criticisms. For instance, the assumption that bright and dull rats differ in their inherited capacity to utilize stimulation is open to question. Furthermore, as pointed out above, possible inadequacies of the Hebb-Williams test may throw doubt on the findings for the bright-enriched rats. Nonetheless, although this theoretical interpretation obviously needs a more adequate foundation, it seems best fitted to account for the experimental data in the light of present neurophysiological knowledge.

SUMMARY

Forty-three rats of the McGill bright and dull strains were used as experimental subjects in an investigation of possible differential effects of enriched and restricted early environments on learning ability.

At 25 days of age, 12 bright rats and 9 dull rats were placed in enriched environments, and 13 brights and 9 dulls were placed in restricted environments. At 65 days of age all animals were introduced to the training and testing procedures of the Hebb-Williams maze, their performances being compared with those of normally reared bright and dull controls.

The bright animals reared in enriched environments showed no improvement in learning ability over bright controls reared under normal laboratory conditions. The dull animals, on the other hand, benefited greatly from the enriched experience and attained a level of performance equal to that of the bright animals. Rearing in restricted environments had converse effects. The dull animals suffered no impairment as compared with dull controls, while the bright animals were retarded to the level of the dulls in learning performance.

Possible neurophysiological explanations are suggested.

REFERENCES

1. Anastasi, Anne. *Psychological testing*. New York: Macmillan, 1954.
2. Beach, F. A., & Janes, J. Effects of early experience upon the behavior of animals. *Psychol. Bull.*, 19545, **51,** 239–263.
3. Bindra, D. Comparative psychology. In *Ann. Rev. Psychol*. Palo Alto, Calif.: Annual Reviews Inc., 1957, **8,** 399–414.
4. Drever, J. The concept of early learning. *Trans. New York Acad. Sci.*, 1955, **17,** 463–469.
5. Hebb, D. O. *The organization of behavior*. New York: Wiley, 1949.
6. Hughes, K. R., & Zubek, J. P. Effect of glutamic acid on the learning ability of bright and dull rats. I. Administration during infancy. *Canad. J. Psychol.*, 1956, **10,** 132–138.
7. Milner, P. M. The cell assembly: Mark II. *Psychol. Rev.*, 1957, **64,** 242–252.
8. Rabinovitch, M. S., & Rosvold, H. E. A closed field intelligence test for rats. *Canad. J. Psychol.*, 1951, **5,** 122–128.
9. Thompson, W. R. Early environment—its importance for later behaviour. Chap. 8 in P. H. Hoch, & J. Zubin (Eds.), *Psychopathology of children*. New York: Grune & Stratton, 1955.

PART 2
Summarize the Results in a Graphic Form

Before you proceed to the questions in Part 3, we suggest that you create a summary of the results in a graph instead of the two-table form used in the article. On the x-axis, mark the three levels of environments they used: *restricted, normal,* and *enriched*. Then, on the y-axis write values ranging from 100 to 200 to represent *mean numbers of errors*. Use the values given in Tables 1 and 2 of the article to plot the performance of the bright (solid line) and dull (dashed line) rats across these three conditions.

Discussion Questions

1. Using your graph, describe and compare the performance of Bright and Dull rats across the three rearing conditions.
2. What was the overall effect of environmental enrichment (contrasted with the restricted condition) on the performances measured in the two lines? How do you explain the fact that the bright and dull rats show the expected genetic effect on problem solving ability only when they have been reared under normal conditions?
3. Add a second graph showing the functions one would obtain for bright and dull rats, if the effects of genes and environments on maze performance were *additive* (i.e., there was no interaction between the two factors).
4. Explain why the results reported by Cooper & Zubek are best interpreted as providing evidence for a multiplicative effect of gene and environments (i.e., of an interaction between the two factors, as opposed to an additive (i.e., independent effects of the two factors).
5. In the modern literature on the topic, several researchers have proposed that the Darwinian notion that *only* genes (not experiences) are transmitted across successive generations is misleading. Instead, they propose that it is not just genes that are transmitted over generations, but genes *and* the specific context that brings about their expression during development (Gottlieb, 1992; Wahlsten, 1998; Ho, 1998). Use the results reported by Cooper & Zubek to substantiate this proposal.
6. It is now well established that chimpanzees and humans share about 97% of their genetic material, yet only humans have the ability to use language. Using your answer to the preceding questions, can you speculate on why this is so?

Selected Readings

Gottlieb, G. (1997). *Synthesizing nature-nurture: prenatal roots of instinctive behavior.* Lawrence Erlbaum Associates: Mahwah, NJ.

Stephens, C. J. & Williams, W. M. (1995). *The nature-nurture debate: the essential readings.* Blackwell: Malden, MA.

Thelen, E. (1992). Development as a dynamic system. *Current Directions In Psychological Science,* 1(6), 189–193.

MODULE 5

IN VITRO FERTILIZATION

In vitro fertilization is a laboratory procedure in which egg fertilization is artificially achieved by uniting the sperm and the egg in a petri dish. Eggs fertilized in this way can then be implanted in the lining of a woman's uterus for potential pregnancy. The questions in this module are intended to facilitate your discussion of the ethical considerations this procedure may raise.

INTRODUCTION

The first human baby conceived through *in vitro* fertilization was born in 1978. Since that time, thousands of babies have been born through the use of this technique, primarily by women whose fallopian tubes are blocked and who cannot conceive a child without the assistance of reproductive technology. Although *in vitro* fertilization is now commonplace, it continues to raise a number of ethical dilemmas.

PART 1
DISCUSSION QUESTIONS

1. Should *in vitro* fertilization ever be allowed as a method of reproduction for infertile couples? Why or why not?
2. Should our government place restrictions on *in vitro* fertilization? If so, what should they be?
3. *In vitro* fertilization is an expensive procedure and is often only affordable by affluent individuals. Should insurance companies cover the cost of the procedure? Why or why not?
4. Because the chances are small that the implantation of a single embryo will result in a pregnancy, doctors often implant multiple embryos. This, of course, dramatically increases the chances of multiple births. Should there be a limit on how many embryos can be implanted? Why or why not?
5. What should happen to the embryos that are not implanted? Should they be discarded or should they be frozen? What should happen to

the embryos if one or both of the parents die while the embryos are in storage?

6. With hormonal treatment, there is currently no limit on the age a healthy woman may carry a child if conceived through the process of *in vitro* fertilization. In fact, a 63-year-old woman in Europe recently gave birth to a child through the use of this technology. Should there be an age restriction placed upon women who use the procedure? Why or why not?

7. When a husband has insufficient or weak sperm, a male donor's sperm may be used to fertilize the wife's egg. Similarly, a wife who cannot produce her own egg may choose to have her husband's sperm united with the egg of a female donor, which can then be implanted in the wife's uterus. In another complex situation, the wife's uterus is not capable of carrying a child to term, so a surrogate mother is solicited to bear the child. In fact, it is conceivable that a child could have at least five "parents": the mother who will raise the child, the father who will raise the child, the donor of the sperm, the donor of the egg, and a surrogate mother who carried the fetus to term. These scenarios highlight a number of concerns. For example, given that an *in vitro* fertilization has taken place, what legal rights should each of the following participants have?

    a. the woman who donated the egg
    b. the man who donated the sperm
    c. the husband of the woman who donated the egg (if not the sperm donor)
    d. the wife of the man who donated the sperm (if not the egg donor)
    e. the woman who accepts implantation of the embryo (if she is paid for this service)
    f. the individuals who pay for the woman to accept implantation
    g. the embryo
    h. the newborn
    i. the physician performing the *in vitro* fertilization

8. How should prospective egg and sperm donors be screened, if at all? What are the problems of having a consumer market for sperm and eggs? Should this market be regulated by the government?

Suggested Readings

Elmer-Dewitt, P. (1991). Making babies, *Time*, September 30, pp. 56–63.

Hopkins, E. (1992). Tales from the baby factory, *New York Times Magazine*, March 15.

Miller A, Raymond, J. (1999). The infertility challenge. *Newsweek. Health for Life*. Special ed., pp. 26–38.

MODULE 6

INFLUENCES ON PRENATAL DEVELOPMENT

In this module you will learn about a number of factors that can negatively influence prenatal development. You will also consider how to reduce their presence at both the individual and societal levels, and will be asked to think about those negative factors that you are currently exposed to.

INTRODUCTION

During the prenatal period, the developing child is vulnerable to a variety of negative influences that may have their origin either in the mother's life style or her health condition, and/or her surrounding environment. These influences include a number agents, called *teratogens* that can potentially affect prenatal development.

The physical health of the mother (e.g., viral diseases), the quality of her nutrition, and her age, all are vitally important to the development of a healthy infant. In addition, her emotional health determines the hormonal levels the developing embryo is exposed to (e.g., high levels of cortisol, the stress hormone), and these, in turn, are affected by the extent of social support she experiences during pregnancy.

Teratogenic agents can be sorted into two categories. The first category includes teratogens that are ingested by the mother. These can be drugs, both legal and illegal, as well as certain herbs. Examples include cigarette smoke, over-the-counter medications, cocaine, and Echinacea. The second category consists of environmental toxins. These toxins are compounds contained in air, water, and structures that the mother comes in contact with. Examples include lead paint or pipes, air pollution, and chemicals encountered in the workplace.

The potential for harm from each of these agents depends on the duration and timing of exposure. In general, the most severe effects on the developing child are observed when exposure occurs in the early stages of pregnancy, with less pronounced effects as the fetus develops. This is largely due to the fact that it is during the early stages of development that the different organs and body structures undergo differentiation (conception to 8 weeks). The impact of teratogens is also influenced by their number and how they may interact with one another.

All sexually active individuals, both males and females, regardless of whether or not they currently intend to conceive, should consider how teratogens and maternal conditions interact to negatively affect prenatal development. There are two compelling reasons for this. First, the presence of some teratogens (e.g., bad nutrition) can be prevented prior to conception by adopting healthy habits early on. Second, and most important, most women do not become aware of a pregnancy (whether it is intentional or accidental) until their menstrual cycle is interrupted, which, typically does not occur until approximately fourth weeks after conception. At this point, mothers who intend to change their habits and to remove teratogenic agents from their environment have already exposed their fetus to these agents during a period critically important to normal development.

Consider the following questions related to your own teratogen exposure. If you are female, answer the questions as though there is the potential that you could become pregnant. If you are male, answer the questions as though you were discussing this with your partner, taking time to realistically consider the teratogens in your life that could affect your partner, and your role in minimizing your child's exposure to teratogens.

■ Discussion Questions

1. Do you have physical, emotional, or social characteristics that could negatively affect your child? What are they? Be sure to think broadly.
2. What are the teratogens present in your life? Of those, which are under your control?
3. What changes in your lifestyle could you make to reduce the negative influences listed in Question 1 and 2? Of those, which changes would you be willing to make now?
4. Consider the role of society in encouraging healthy development, prevention and policy. Think about specific ways in which the following institutions can affect maternal characteristics and the presence of teratogens from any source during pregnancy.
    a. schools
    b. the workplace
    c. local government
    d. federal government
    e. the medical community

■ Selected Readings

Barr, H. M., Streissguth, A. P., Darby, B. L., & Sampson, P. D. (1990). Prenatal exposure to alcohol, caffeine, tobacco, and aspirin: effects on fine and gross motor performance in 4-year-old children. *Developmental Psychology, 26*, p. 339.

Narod, S. A., de Sanjose, S., & Victora, C. (1991). Coffee during pregnancy: a reproductive hazard? *American Journal of Obstetrics and Gynecology, 164*, 1109.

MODULE 7

THE MOZART EFFECT

Much interest has been paid to a recently identified phenomenon known as *The Mozart Effect*. This module examines the research underlying The Mozart Effect in order to understand its origins. It will then follow the Mozart Effect's path to popularity, due in part to popular press journals, and conclude with an examination of how it has affected public policy.

INTRODUCTION

The Mozart Effect, as it is popularly defined, refers to the hypothesis that listening to classical music increases an individual's cognitive abilities. The roots of research into this phenomenon begin in animal research. Rosenzweig (1966) placed rats from the same litters into either an enriched environment (with other rats and novel toys), or an impoverished environment (alone with bedding only). After three months of differential exposure to these environments, the rats were sacrificed and the brains of the two groups of rats were compared. The rats that were raised in the enriched condition had brains that weighed more and had neurons that were more richly interconnected.

PART 1
REQUIRED READING

In the context of a general interest on how the environment may affect brain development, the findings reported by Rosenzweig (1966) led another group of researchers, Rauscher, Shaw, and Ky (1993), to examine how exposure to classical music by the composer Mozart may affect intelligence development in the young rat. Read their research report and pay special attention to the theory that guided their choice of methods, their findings, and their interpretation.

Music and Spatial Task Performance

Reprinted by permission from Nature, *Vol. 365. Copyright © 1993 Macmillan Publishers Ltd.*

SIR—There are correlational[1], historical[2] and anecdotal[3] relationships between music cognition and other 'higher brain functions', but no causal relationship has been demonstrated between music cognition and cognitions pertaining to abstract operations such as mathematical or spatial reasoning. We performed an experiment in which students were each given three sets of standard IQ spatial reasoning tasks; each task was preceded by 10 minutes of (1) listening to Mozart's sonata for two pianos in D major, K488; (2) listening to a relaxation tape; or (3) silence. Performance was improved for those tasks immediately following the first condition compared to the second two.

Thirty-six college students participated in all three listening conditions. Immediately following each listening condition, the student's spatial reasoning skills were tested using the Stanford–Binet intelligence scale.[4] The mean standard age scores (SAS) for the three listening conditions are shown in the figure. The music condition yielded a mean SAS of 57.56; the mean SAS for the relaxation condition was 54.61 and the mean score for the silent condition was 54.00. To assess the impact of these scores, we 'translated' them to spatial IQ scores of 119, 111 and 110, respectively. Thus, the IQs of subjects participating in the music condition were 8–9 points above their IQ scores in the other two conditions. A one-factor (listening condition) repeated measures analysis of variance (ANOVA) performed on SAS revealed that subjects performed better on the abstract/spatial reasoning tests after listening to Mozart than after listening to either the relaxation tape or to nothing ($F_{2,35} = 7.08; P = 0.002$). The music condition differed significantly from both the relaxation and the silence conditions (Scheffe's $t = 3.41, P = 0.002; t = 3.67, P = 0.0008$, two-tailed, respectively). The relaxation and silence conditions did not differ ($t = 0.795; P = 0.432$, two-tailed). Pulse rates were taken before and after each listening condition. A two-factor (listening condition and time of pulse measure) repeated measures ANOVA revealed no interaction or main effects for pulse, thereby excluding arousal as an obvious cause. We

FIGURE

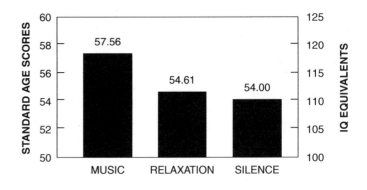

Standard age scores for each of the three listening conditions.

Testing procedure. In the music condition, the subject listened to 10 min of the Mozart piece. The relaxation condition required the subject to listen to 10 min of relaxation instructions designed to lower blood pressure. The silence condition required the subject to sit in silence for 10 min. One of three abstract reasoning tests taken from the Stanford–Binet intelligence scale[4] was given after each of the listening conditions. The abstract spatial reasoning tasks consisted of a pattern analysis test, a multiple-choice matrices test and a multiple-choice paper-folding and cutting test. For our sample, these three tasks correlated at the 0.01 level of significance. We were thus able to treat them as equal measures of abstract reasoning ability.

Scoring. Raw scores were calculated by subtracting the number of items failed from the highest item number administered. These were then converted to SAS using the Stanford–Binet's SAS conversion table of normalized standard scores with a mean set at 50 and a standard deviation of 8. IQ equivalents were calculated by first multiplying each SAS by 3 (the number of subtests required by the Stanford–Binet for calculating IQs). We then used their area score conversion table, designed to have a mean of 100 and a standard deviation of 16, to obtain SAS IQ equivalents.

found no order effects for either condition presentation or task, nor any experimenter effect.

The enhancing effect of the music condition is temporal, and does not extend beyond the 10–15 minute period during which subjects were engaged in each spatial task. Inclusion of a delay period (as a variable) between the music listening condition and the testing period would allow us quantitatively to determine the presence of a decay constant. It would also be interesting to vary the listening time to optimize the enhancing effect, and to examine whether other measures of general intelligence (verbal reasoning, quantitative reasoning and short-term memory) would be similarly facilitated. Because we used only one musical sample of one composer, various other compositions and musical styles should also be examined. We predict that music lacking complexity or which is repetitive may interfere with, rather than enhance, abstract reasoning. Also, as musicians may process music in a different way from non-musicians, it would be interesting to compare these two groups.

Frances H. Rauscher
Gordon L. Shaw*
Katherine N. Ky
*Center for the Neurobiology
of Learning and Memory,
University of California,
Irvine, California 92717, USA*
***Also at Department of Physics**

FOOTNOTES

1. Hassier, M., Birbaumer, N. & Feil, A. *Psychol. Music* **13**, 99–113 (1985).
2. Altman, G. J. *Greek Geometry from Thales to Euclid* p. 23 (Arno, New York, 1976).
3. Cranberg, L. D. & Albert M. L. in *The Exceptional Brain* (eds. Obler, L. K. & Fein, D.) 156 (Guilford, New York, 1988).
4. Thorndike, R. L., Hagen, E. P., & Sattler, J. M. *The Stanford–Binet Scale of Intelligence* (Riverside, Chicago, 1986).

PART 2
■ REQUIRED READING

The research of Rauscher et al (1993) and other similar studies found their way to the public via the popular press in 2000. *Time* magazine ran a cover story detailing ways for parents to *build better brains* by enhancing the richness of their children's environment early in life. This article was the first of many in the popular press to recommend methods of enhancing children's cognitive development through advanced toys, learning games, and through listening to music. These articles caused a stir among America's parents. Parents rushed to purchase classical music in order to *educate* their infants, and entrepreneurs began marketing compact disks aimed at these hopeful parents. Read this *Time* article and consider the conclusions that the author has drawn in relation to what you know of the research that underlies this piece.

FERTILE MINDS

From birth, a baby's brain cells proliferate wildly, making connections that may shape a lifetime of experience. The first three years are critical.

J. Madeleine Nash

© *1997 Time Inc. reprinted by permission.*

Rat-a-tat-tat, rat-a-tat-tat, rat-a-tat-tat. If scientists could eavesdrop on the brain of a human embryo 10, maybe 12 weeks after conception, they would hear an astonishing racket. Inside the womb, long before light first strikes the retina of the eye or the earliest dreamy images flicker through the cortex, nerve cells in the developing brain crackle with purposeful activity. Like teenagers with telephones, cells in one neighborhood of the brain are calling friends in another, and these cells are calling their friends, and they keep calling one another over and over again, "almost," says neurobiologist Carla Shatz of the University of California, Berkeley, "as if they were autodialing."

But these neurons—as the long, wiry cells that carry electrical messages through the nervous system and the brain are called—are not transmitting signals in scattershot fashion. That would produce a featureless static, the sort of noise picked up by a radio tuned between stations. On the contrary, evidence is growing that the staccato bursts of electricity that form those distinctive rat-a-tat-tats arise from coordinated waves of neural activity, and that those pulsing waves, like currents shifting sand on the ocean floor, actually change the shape of the brain, carving mental circuits into patterns that over time will enable the newborn infant to perceive a father's voice, a mother's touch, a shiny mobile twirling over the crib.

Of all the discoveries that have poured out of neuroscience labs in recent years, the finding that the electrical activity of brain cells changes the physical structure of the brain is perhaps the most breathtaking. For the rhythmic firing of neurons is no longer assumed to be a by-product of building the brain but essential to the process, and it begins, scientists have established, well before birth. A brain is not a computer. Nature does not cobble it together, then turn it on. No, the brain begins working long before it is finished. And the same processes that wire the brain before birth, neuroscientists are finding, also drive the explosion of learning that occurs immediately afterward.

At birth a baby's brain contains 100 billion neurons, roughly as many nerve cells as there are stars in the Milky Way. Also in place are a trillion glial cells, named after the Greek word for glue, which form a kind of honeycomb that protects and nourishes the neurons. But while the brain contains virtually all the nerve cells it will ever have, the pattern of wiring between them has yet to stabilize. Up to this point, says Shatz, "what the brain has done is lay out circuits that are its best guess about what's required for vision, for language, for whatever." And now it is up to neural activity—no longer spontaneous, but driven by a flood of sensory experiences—to take this rough blueprint and progressively refine it.

During the first years of life, the brain undergoes a series of extraordinary changes. Starting shortly after birth, a baby's brain, in a display of biological exuberance, produces trillions more connections between neurons that it can possibly use. Then, through a process that resembles Darwinian competition, the brain eliminates connections, or synapses, that are seldom or never used. The excess synapses in a child's brain undergo a draconian pruning, starting around the age of 10 or earlier, leaving behind a mind whose patterns of emotion and thought are, for better or worse, unique.

Deprived of a stimulating environment, a child's brain suffers. Researchers at Baylor College of Medicine, for example, have found that children who don't play much or are rarely touched develop brains 20% to 30% smaller than normal for their age. Laboratory animals provide another provocative parallel. Not only do young rats reared in toy-strewn cages exhibit more complex behavior than rats confined to sterile, uninteresting boxes, researchers at the University of Illinois at Urbana-Champaign have found, but the brains of these rats contain as many as 25% more synapses per neuron. Rich experiences, in other words, really do produce rich brains.

The new insights into brain development are more than just interesting science. They have profound implications for parents and policymakers. In an age when mothers and fathers are increasingly pressed for time—and may already be feeling guilty about how many hours they spend away from their children—the results coming out of the labs are likely to increase concerns about leaving very young children in the care of others. For the data underscore the importance of hands-on parenting, of finding the time to cuddle a baby, talk with a toddler and provide infants with stimulating experiences.

The new insights have begun to infuse new passion into the political debate over early education and day care. There is an urgent need, say child-development experts, for preschool programs designed to boost the brain power of youngsters born into impoverished rural and inner-city households. Without such programs, they warn, the current drive to curtail welfare costs by pushing mothers with infants and toddlers into the work force may well backfire. "There is a time scale to brain development, and the most important year is the first," notes Frank Newman, president of the Education Commission of the States. By the age of three, a child who is neglected or abused bears marks that, if not indelible, are exceedingly difficult to erase.

But the new research offers hope as well. Scientists have found that the brain during the first years of life is so malleable that very young children who suffer strokes or injuries that wipe out an entire hemisphere can still mature into highly functional adults. Moreover, it is becoming increasingly clear that well-designed preschool programs can help many children overcome glaring deficits in their home environment. With appropriate therapy, say researchers, even serious disorders like dyslexia may be treatable. While inherited problems may place certain children at greater risk than others, says Dr. Harry Chugani, a pediatric neurologist at Wayne State University in Detroit, that is no excuse for ignoring the environment's power to remodel the brain. "We may not do much to change what happens before birth, but we can change what happens after a baby is born," he observes.

Strong evidence that activity changes the brain began accumulating in the 1970s. But only recently have researchers had tools powerful enough to reveal the precise mechanisms by which those changes are brought about. Neural activity triggers a biochemical cascade that reaches all the way to the nucleus of cells and the coils of DNA that encode specific genes. In fact, two of the genes affected by neural activity in embryonic fruit flies, neurobiologist Corey Goodman and his colleagues at Berkeley reported late last year, are identical to those that other studies have linked to learning and memory. How thrilling, exclaims Goodman, how intellectually satisfying that the snippets of DNA that embryos use to build their brains are the very same ones that will later allow adult organisms to process and store new information.

As researchers explore the once hidden links between brain activity and brain structure, they are beginning to construct a sturdy bridge over the chasm that previously separated genes from the environment. Experts now agree that a baby does not come into the world as a genetically pre-programmed automaton or a blank slate at the mercy of the environment, but arrives as something much more interesting. For this reason the debate that engaged countless generations of philosophers—whether nature or nurture calls the shots—no longer interests most scientists. They are much too busy chronicling the myriad ways in which genes and the environment interact. "It's not a competition," says Dr. Stanley Greenspan, a psychiatrist at George Washington University. "It's a dance."

THE IMPORTANCE OF GENES

That dance begins at around the third week of gestation, when a thin layer of cells in the developing embryo performs an origami-like trick, folding inward to give rise to a fluid-filled cylinder known as the neural tube. As cells in the neural tube proliferate at the astonishing rate of 250,000 a minute, the brain and spinal cord assemble themselves in a series of tightly choreographed steps. Nature is the dominant partner during this phase of development, but nurture plays a vital supportive role. Changes in the environment of the womb—whether caused by maternal malnutrition, drug abuse or a viral infection—can wreck the clockwork precision of the neural assembly line. Some forms of epilepsy, mental retardation, autism and schizophrenia appear to be the results of developmental processes gone awry.

But what awes scientists who study the brain, what still stuns them, is not that things occasionally go wrong in the developing brain but that so much of the time they go right. This is all the more remarkable, says Berkeley's Shatz, as the central nervous system of an embryo is not a miniature of the adult system but more like a tadpole that gives rise to a frog. Among other things, the cells produced in the neural tube must migrate to distant locations and accurately lay down the connections that link one part of the brain to another. In addition, the embryonic brain must construct a variety of temporary structures, including the neural tube, that will, like a tadpole's tail, eventually disappear.

What biochemical magic underlies this incredible metamorphosis? The instructions programmed into the genes, of course. Scientists have recently discovered, for instance, that a gene nicknamed "sonic hedgehog" (after the popular videogame Sonic the Hedgehog) determines the fate of neurons in the spinal cord and the brain. Like a strong scent carried by the wind, the protein encoded by the hedgehog gene (so called because in its absence, fruit-fly embryos sprout a coat of prickles) diffuses outward from the cells that produce it, becoming fainter and fainter. Columbia University neurobiologist Thomas Jessell has found that it takes middling concentrations of this potent morphing factor to produce a motor neuron and lower concentrations to make an interneuron (a cell that relays signals to other neurons, instead of to muscle fibers, as motor neurons do).

Scientists are also beginning to identify some of the genes that guide neurons in their long migrations. Consider the problem faced by neurons destined to become part of the cerebral cortex. Because they arise relatively late in the development of the mammalian brain, billions of these cells must push and shove their way through dense colonies established by earlier migrants. "It's as if the entire population of the East Coast decided to move en masse to the West Coast," marvels Yale University neuroscientist Dr. Pasko Rakic, and marched through Cleveland, Chicago and Denver to get there.

But of all the problems the growing nervous system must solve, the most daunting is posed by the wiring itself. After birth, when the number of connections explodes, each of the brain's billions of neurons will forge links to thousands of others. First they must spin out a web of wirelike fibers known as axons (which transmit signals) and dendrites (which receive them). The objective is to form a synapse, the gaplike structure over which the axon of one neuron beams a signal to the dendrites of another. Before this can happen, axons and dendrites must almost touch. And while the short, bushy dendrites don't have to travel very far, axons—the heavy-duty cables of the nervous system—must traverse distances that are the microscopic equivalent of miles.

What guides an axon on its incredible voyage is a "growth cone," a creepy, crawly sprout that looks something like an amoeba. Scientists have known about growth cones since the turn of the century. What they didn't know until recently was that growth cones come equipped with the molecular equivalent of sonar and radar. Just as instruments in a submarine or airplane scan the environment for signals, so molecules arrayed on the surface of growth cones search their surroundings for the presence of certain proteins. Some of these proteins, it turns out, are attractants that pull the growth cones toward them, while others are repellents that push them away.

THE FIRST STIRRINGS

Up to this point, genes have controlled the unfolding of the brain. As soon as axons make their first connections, however, the nerves begin to fire, and what they do starts to matter more and more. In essence, say scientists, the developing nervous system has strung the equivalent of telephone trunk lines between the right neighborhoods in the right cities. Now it has to sort out which wires belong to which house, a problem that cannot be solved by genes alone for reasons that boil down to simple arithmetic. Eventually, Berkeley's Goodman estimates, a human brain must forge quadrillions of connections. But there are only 100,000 genes in human DNA. Even though half these genes—some 50,000—appear to be dedicated to constructing and maintaining the nervous system, he observes, that's not enough to specify more than a tiny fraction of the connections required by a fully functioning brain.

In adult mammals, for example, the axons that connect the brain's visual system arrange themselves in striking layers and columns that reflect the division between the left eye and the right. But these axons start out as scrambled as a bowl of spaghetti, according to Michael Stryker, chairman of the physiology department at the University of California at San Francisco. What sorts out the mess, scientists have established, is neural activity. In a series of experiments viewed as classics by scientists in the field, Berkeley's Shatz chemically blocked neural activity in embryonic cats. The result? The axons that connect neurons in the retina of the eye to the brain never formed the left eye–right eye geometry needed to support vision.

But no recent finding has intrigued researchers more than the results reported in October by Corey Goodman and his Berkeley colleagues. In studying a deceptively simple problem—how axons from motor neurons in the fly's central nerve cord establish connections with muscle cells in its limbs—the Berkeley researchers made an unexpected discovery. They knew there was a gene that keeps bundles of axons together as they race toward their muscle-cell targets. What they discovered was that the electrical activity produced by neurons inhibited this gene, dramatically increasing the number of connections the axons made. Even more intriguing, the signals amplified the activity of a second gene—a gene called CREB.

The discovery of the CREB amplifier, more than any other, links the developmental processes that occur before birth to those that continue long after. For the twin processes of memory and learning in adult animals, Columbia University neurophysiologist Eric Kandel has shown, rely on the CREB molecule. When Kandel blocked the activity of CREB in giant snails, their brains changed in ways that suggested that they could still learn but could remember what they learned for only a short period of time. Without CREB, it seems, snails—and by extension, more developed animals like humans—can form no long-term memories. And without long-term memories, it is hard to imagine that infant brains could ever master more than rudimentary skills. "Nurture is important," says Kandel. "But nurture works through nature."

EXPERIENCE KICKS IN

When a baby is born, it can see and hear and smell and respond to touch, but only dimly. The brain stem, a primitive region that controls vital functions like heartbeat and breathing, has completed its wiring. Elsewhere the connections between neurons are wispy and weak. But over the first few months of life, the brain's higher centers explode with new synapses. And as dendrites and axons swell with buds and branches like trees in spring, metabolism soars. By the age of two, a child's brain contains twice as many synapses and consumes twice as much energy as the brain of a normal adult.

University of Chicago pediatric neurologist Dr. Peter Huttenlocher has chronicled this extraordinary epoch in brain development by autopsying the brains of infants and young children who have died unexpectedly. The number of synapses in one layer of the visual cortex, Huttenlocher reports, rises from around 2,500 per neuron at birth to as many as 18,000 about six months later. Other regions of the cortex score similarly spectacular increases but on slightly different schedules. And while these microscopic connections between nerve fibers continue to form throughout life, they reach their highest average densities (15,000 synapses per neuron) at around the age of two and remain at that level until the age of 10 or 11.

This profusion of connections lends the growing brain exceptional flexibility and resilience. Consider the case of 13-year-old Brandi Binder, who developed such severe epilepsy that surgeons at UCLA had to remove the entire right side of her cortex when she was six. Binder lost virtually all the control she had established over muscles on the left side of her body, the side controlled by the right side of the brain. Yet today, after years of therapy ranging from leg lifts to math and music drills, Binder is an A student at the Holmes Middle School in Colorado Springs, Colorado. She loves music, math and art—skills usually associated with the right half of the brain. And while Binder's recuperation is not 100%—for example, she has never regained the use of her left arm—it comes close. Says UCLA pediatric neurologist Dr. Donald Shields: "If there's a way to compensate, the developing brain will find it."

What wires a child's brain, say neuroscientists—or rewires it after physical trauma—is repeated experience. Each time a baby tries to touch a tantalizing object or gazes intently at a face or listens to a lullaby, tiny bursts of electricity shoot through the brain, knitting neurons into circuits as well defined as those etched onto silicon chips. The results are those behavioral mileposts that never cease to delight and awe parents. Around the age of two months, for example, the motor-control centers of the brain develop to the point that infants can suddenly reach out and grab a near-by object. Around the age of four months, the cortex begins to refine the connections needed for depth perception and binocular vision. And around the age of 12 months, the speech centers of the brain are poised to produce what is perhaps the most magical moment of childhood: the first word that marks the flowering of language.

When the brain does not receive the right information—or shuts it out—the result can be devastating. Some children who display early signs of autism, for example, retreat from the world because they are hypersensitive to sensory stimulation, others because their senses are underactive and provide them with too little information. To be effective, then, says George Washington University's Greenspan, treatment must target the underlying condition, protecting some children from disorienting noises and lights, providing others with attention-grabbing stimulation. But when parents and therapists collaborate in an intensive effort to reach these abnormal brains, writes Greenspan in a new book, *The Growth of the Mind* (Addison-Wesley, 1997), three-year-olds who begin the descent into the autistic's limited universe can sometimes be snatched back.

Indeed, parents are the brain's first and most important teachers. Among other things, they appear to help babies learn by adopting the rhythmic, high-pitched speaking style known as Parentese. When speaking to babies, Stanford University psychologist Anne Fernald has found, mothers and fathers from many cultures change their speech patterns in the same peculiar ways. "They put their faces very close to the child," she reports. "They use shorter utterances, and they speak in an unusually melodious fashion." The heart rate of infants increases while listening to Parentese, even Parentese delivered in a foreign language. Moreover, Fernald says, Parentese appears to hasten the process of connecting words to the objects they denote. Twelve-month-olds, directed to "look at the ball" in Parentese, direct their eyes to the correct picture more frequently than when the instruction is delivered in normal English.

In some ways the exaggerated, vowel-rich sounds of Parentese appear to resemble the choice morsels fed to hatchlings by adult birds. The University of Washington's Patricia Kuhl and her colleagues have conditioned dozens of newborns to turn their heads when they detect the *ee* sounds emitted by American parents, vs. the *eu* favored by doting Swedes. Very young babies, says Kuhl, invariably perceive slight variations in pronunciation as totally different sounds. But by the age of six months, American babies no longer react when they hear variants of *ee,* and Swedish babies have become impervious to differences in *eu*. "It's as though their brains have formed little magnets," says Kuhl, "and all the sounds in the vicinity are swept in."

TUNED TO DANGER

Even more fundamental, says Dr. Bruce Perry of Baylor College of Medicine in Houston, is the role parents play in setting up the neural circuitry that helps children regulate their responses to stress. Children who are physically abused early in life, he observes, develop brains that are exquisitely tuned to danger. At the slightest threat, their hearts race, their stress hormones surge and their brains anxiously track the nonverbal cues that might signal the next attack. Because the brain develops in sequence, with more primitive structures stabilizing their connections first, early abuse is particularly damaging. Says Perry: "Experience is the chief architect of the brain." And because these early experiences of stress form a kind of template around which later brain development is organized, the changes they create are all the more pervasive.

Emotional deprivation early in life has a similar effect. For six years University of Washington psychologist Geraldine Dawson and her colleagues have monitored the brain-wave patterns of children born to mothers who were diagnosed as suffering from depression. As infants, these children showed markedly reduced activity in the left frontal lobe, an area of the brain that serves as a center for joy and other light-hearted emotions. Even more telling, the patterns of brain activity displayed by these children closely tracked the ups and downs of their mother's depression. At the age of three, children whose mothers were more severely depressed or whose depression lasted longer continued to show abnormally low readings.

Strikingly, not all the children born to depressed mothers develop these aberrant brain-wave patterns, Dawson has found. What accounts for the difference appears to be the emotional tone of the exchanges between mother and child. By scrutinizing hours of videotape that show depressed mothers interacting with their babies, Dawson has attempted to identify the links between maternal behavior and children's brains. She found that mothers who were disengaged, irritable or impatient had babies with sad brains. But depressed mothers who managed to rise above their melancholy, lavishing their babies with attention and indulging in playful games, had children with brain activity of a considerably more cheerful cast.

When is it too late to repair the damage wrought by physical and emotional abuse or neglect? For a time, at least, a child's brain is extremely forgiving. If a mother snaps out of her depression before her child is a year old, Dawson has found, brain activity in the left frontal lobe quickly picks up. However, the ability to rebound declines markedly as a child grows older. Many scientists believe that in the first few years of childhood there are a number of critical or sensitive periods, or "windows," when the brain demands certain types of input in order to create or stabilize certain long-lasting structures.

For example, children who are born with a cataract will become permanently blind in that eye if the clouded lens is not promptly removed. Why? The brain's visual centers require sensory stimulus—in this case the stimulus provided by light hitting the retina of the eye—to maintain their still tentative connections. More controversially, many linguists believe that language skills unfold according to a strict, biologically defined timetable. Children, in their view, resemble certain species of birds that cannot master their song unless they hear it sung at an early age. In zebra finches the window for acquiring the appropriate song opens 25 to 30 days after hatching and shuts some 50 days later.

WINDOWS OF OPPORTUNITY

With a few exceptions, the windows of opportunity in the human brain do not close quite so abruptly. There appears to be a series of windows for developing language. The window for acquiring syntax may close as early as five or six years of age, while the window for adding new words may never close. The ability to learn a second language is highest between birth and the age of six, then undergoes a steady and inexorable decline. Many adults still manage to learn new languages, but usually only after great struggle.

The brain's greatest growth spurt, neuroscientists have now confirmed, draws to a close around the age of 10, when the balance between synapse creation and atrophy abruptly shifts. Over the next several years, the brain will ruthlessly destroy its weakest synapses, preserving only those that have been magically transformed by experience. This magic, once again, seems to be encoded in the genes. The ephemeral bursts of electricity that travel through the brain, creating everything from visual images and pleasurable sensations to dark dreams and wild thoughts, ensure the survival of synapses by stimulating genes that promote the release of powerful growth factors and suppressing genes that encode for synapse-destroying enzymes.

By the end of adolescence, around the age of 18, the brain has declined in plasticity but increased in power. Talents and latent tendencies that have been nurtured are ready to blossom. The experiences that drive neural activity, says Yale's Rakic, are like a sculptor's chisel or a dressmaker's shears, conjuring up form from a lump of stone or a length of cloth. The presence of extra material expands the range of possibilities, but cutting away the extraneous is what makes art. "It is the overproduction of synaptic connections followed by their loss that leads to patterns in the brain," says neuroscientist William Greenough of the University of Illinois at Urbana–Champaign. Potential for greatness may be encoded in the genes, but whether that potential is realized as a gift for mathematics, say, or a brilliant criminal mind depends on patterns etched by experience in those critical early years.

Psychiatrists and educators have long recognized the value of early experience. But their observations have until now been largely anecdotal. What's so exciting, says Matthew Melmed, executive director of Zero to Three, a nonprofit organization devoted to highlighting the importance of the first three years of life, is that modern neuroscience is providing the hard, quantifiable evidence that was missing earlier. "Because you can see the results under a microscope or in a PET scan," he observes, "it's become that much more convincing."

What lessons can be drawn from the new findings? Among other things, it is clear that foreign languages should be taught in elementary school, if not before. That remedial education may be more effective at the age of three or four than at nine or 10. That good, affordable day care is not a luxury or a fringe benefit for welfare mothers and working parents but essential brain food for the next generation. For while new synapses continue to form throughout life, and even adults continually refurbish their minds through reading and learning, never again will the brain be able to master new skills so readily or rebound from setbacks so easily.

Rat-a-tat-tat. Rat-a-tat-tat. Rat-a-tat-tat. Just last week, in the U.S. alone, some 77,000 newborns began the miraculous process of wiring their brains for a lifetime of learning. If parents and policymakers don't pay attention to the conditions under which this delicate process takes place, we will all suffer the consequences—starting around the year 2010.

PART 3
REQUIRED READING

The final chapter of this story brings us to the mansion of Governor Zell Miller in Atlanta, Georgia. Governor Miller argued for the creation of a state-funded program through which all new mothers in Georgia would receive a classical music CD prior to leaving the hospital. Miller's program aimed to provide parents with the means to enhance the brain development of their children. Read the statement that outlines the Governor's goal in creating the program. Pay close attention to his information sources. Then, make your own evaluation of his decision in light of what you have learned in your reading of the preceding two articles by Rauscher et al. (1993) and Nash (1997).

MOZART FOR THE MASSES

From Daily InSCIght, *Posted January 20, 1998. Copyright © 1998 by American Association for the Advancement of Science. Reprinted by permission.*

Georgia governor Zell Miller has gotten so much positive feedback from his proposal to harness the "Mozart effect" for Georgia's newborns—that is, expose them to classical music to try to improve early brain development—that private donors are ready to fund the project themselves. But the scientists whose work has influenced Miller's ideas are skeptical that his plan will work.

Miller, a Democrat, has proposed that the state allocate $105,000 in next year's budget to buy a classical music tape or CD for every baby born in Georgia—more than 100,000 a year. The reason? "No one questions that listening to music at a very early age affects the spatial, temporal reasoning that underlies math and engineering and even chess," Miller told the state legislature on 15 January. To press home his point, he treated listeners to an excerpt from Beethoven's *Ode to Joy*.

Miller's conclusions about childhood brain plasticity are drawn heavily from a *Time* cover story on infant brain development that appeared last February, says his press secretary, Rick Dent. His faith in the power of music is based on two pieces of research done at the University of California, Irvine. The first, reported last year in *Nature,* found that listening to Mozart briefly raised the intelligence quotients* of college students. The second (*Science,* 28 November 1997, p. 1621) found that the spatial skills of 3-year-olds benefited from keyboard music lessons.

The Irvine researchers, who were not consulted by the governor, are skeptical about the plan.

---

*Definitions from the AP Dictionary of Science and Technology

According to psychologist Frances Rauscher, now at the University of Wisconsin, Oshkosh, "None of our studies show that listening casually [as opposed to taking lessons] has any effect at all for children."

Dent, however, says the governor's office has been "flooded with calls" from the press and from health personnel, researchers, and businesses. So far, four recording companies have offered to donate tapes or CDs to the package containing pamphlets and Pampers that new mothers take home from the hospital. With this level of support, says Dent, "we think we can get it up and running by April first."

PART 4
Discussion Questions

Now that you have read about a piece of empirical research, its popularization through the popular media, and its eventual translation into public policy, consider the following questions related to the translation of knowledge across these three steps.

1. What conclusions did Rauscher et al. (1993) draw on the basis of their research? Did the authors express any reservations concerning the generalizability of their findings? What strengths and weaknesses do you see in their study?

2. What aspects of their empirical findings were subsequently emphasized or de-emphasized in the *Time* article? In your opinion, what portions of the article represent an accurate portrayal, and what portions stretch the data too far?

3. Do you feel that Governor Miller's program will be effective? What are the pros and cons of his program?

4. It is apparent from the example of the Mozart Effect that in the translation of empirical findings into public knowledge, there is always the risk of misinterpretation. How much of the responsibility for maintaining the integrity of the findings falls to the original researcher? The popular press? Politicians and public leaders?

5. As a member of the news-consuming public, does this exercise change your opinion of what you read in magazines or hear on television? What is your responsibility for verifying the information you receive through the media?

Selected Readings

Bruer, J. T. (1999). *The Myth of the First Three Years*. Free Press: New York, NY.

Greenough, W. T., Black, J. E., & Wallace, C. S. (1987). Experience and brain development. *Child Development, 58*, 539–559.

Larkin, M. (1999). Mozart effect comes under strong fire. *The Lancet, 354*, 749.

Rosenzweig, M. R. (1966). Environmental complexity, cerebral change, and behavior. *American Psychologist, 21*, 321–332.

MODULE 8

COG—THE HUMANOID ROBOT

Beginning in the early 1990's, research on artificial intelligence has tried to create information processing systems that not only mimic the results of human cognitive activity, but also the very processes by which the human brain achieves these results. In recognition of the fact that the human brain does not come into the world fully equipped with adult capacities, more recent attempts in artificial intelligence research have consisted in trying to create machines that have to *develop* in order to perform adult-like functions. This module brings to your attention a long-term project aimed at designing and building a humanoid robot that has to build its capacities through development. You will read an article published in a popular scientific magazine that gives a general overview of this project. The questions that follow are provided as a starting point for a discussion of what, if anything, can be learned about child development through this sort of project.

INTRODUCTION

MIT's Artificial Intelligence Lab has undertaken a long-term project to design and build a humanoid robot. This robot, named Cog, has a trunk, a head, two eyes, two arms, and hands and has sensory systems that imitate those of humans, including visual, auditory, tactile, and vestibular systems. Cog has been designed to go through a period of artificial infancy, in that it learns by trial-and-error, rather than through built-in programs, how its own body works and how it can use its body to act upon external objects. If you are already aware of the Piagetian theory, you know that the organization of the body is a necessary first step to generate intelligent actions aimed at the environment. The ultimate goal of the Cog project is to make a robot that can interact with human beings in an adaptable manner and also take care of itself. As such, the researchers also hope that Cog will be able to learn a rudimentary language. Cog has software that makes it likely that it will be able to discriminate human speech sounds and the people that produce them, and Cog's creators are currently working on giving Cog a voice.

According to the Guinness World Records 2000, Cog is the most intelligent robot in the world. As of now, Cog can locate and fixate on moving objects, it can reach out and touch objects, it can nod and shake its head, it can recognize eyes and faces, it can play with a Slinky toy, and it can rotate a crank.

PART 1
Required Reading

Here's Looking at You

A disarming robot starts to act up

Tim Beardsley

Reprinted with permission. Copyright © 1999 by Scientific American, Inc. All rights reserved.

Parties have a way of generating outrageous ideas. Most don't survive the night, but a scheme that bubbled to the surface at a 1992 event held by Rodney A. Brooks of the Massachusetts Institute of Technology is changing the way researchers think about thinking. Brooks, the head of M.I.T.'s artificial intelligence laboratory, was celebrating the switch-on date of the fictitious Hal 9000 computer, which appeared in the movie *2001: A Space Odyssey*. As he reflected that no silicon brain could yet rival Hal's slick mendacity, he was seized by the notion of building a humanoid robot based on biological principles, rather than on conventional approaches to robot design.

The robot, known as Cog, started to take shape in the summer of 1993. The project, which was initially to last five years, is intended to reveal problems that emerge in trying to design a humanoid machine and thereby elucidate principles of human cognition. Instead of being programmed with detailed information about its environment and then calculating how to achieve a set goal—the modus operandi of industrial robots—Cog learns about itself and its environment by trial and error. Brooks says that although there are no near-term practical goals for Cog technology, it has stimulated "a bunch" of papers.

Central to the plan was that the robot should (unlike Hal) look and move something like a human being, to encourage people to interact with it. Tufts University philosopher Daniel C. Dennett, an informal adviser to the fluid group of M.I.T. researchers who have worked on Cog, has stated that the machine "will be conscious if we get done all the things we've got written down." Another principle guiding the project was that it should not include a preplanned, or explicit, internal "model" of the world. Rather the changes in Cog as it learns are, in the team's words, "meaningless without interaction with the outside world."

A little after the five-year mark, not even the most enthusiastic fan could argue that Cog is conscious. Yet it is also clear that the exercise of building it has highlighted some intriguing observations.

One day last fall Brian Scassellati and Cynthia Breazeal of Brooks's department exhibited some of Cog's tricks. The machine's upper-torso humanoid form is irresistibly reminiscent of C3PO of *Star Wars* fame. It has learned how to turn to fixate on a moving object, first switching its swiveling eyes, then moving its whole head to catch up. Cog will imitate a nod and reach out to touch things with strikingly lifelike arm movements. The movements have a fluidity not usually associated with machines, because they are driven by a system that has learned to exploit the limbs' natural dynamics.

Cog's mechanical facility is revealed in the way it quickly picks up the timing needed to play with a slinky toy attached to its hands or spontaneously rotates a crank. According to Brooks, a major milestone in Cog's development—that of having multiple systems working together simultaneously—was set to be achieved within the next few months.

Plans are under way to provide the robot with more tactile sensors, a better controlled posture and the ability to distinguish different sound sources. Cog should then be able to associate a voice with a human being in its visual field. There are no plans to add a premade speech-recognition capability, because that would violate the guiding philosophy that Cog should learn on its own.

An expandable stack of high-speed processors gives Cog enough computing power to build on its current skills, Brooks explains. Yet even in its present, simple incarnation, Cog can elicit unexpected behavior from humans. Breazeal once found herself taking turns with Cog passing an eraser between them, a game she had not planned but which the situation seemed to invite.

Breazeal is now studying emotional interactions with a disembodied Cog-type head equipped with expressive mobile eyelids, ears and a jaw. This robot, called Kismet, might yield insights that will expand Cog's mental horizons. Kismet, unlike Cog, has built-in drives for social activity, stimulation and fatigue and can create expressions of happiness, sadness, anger, fear or disgust. Like a baby, it can manipulate a soft-hearted human into providing it with a companionable level of interaction.

It is clear that Cog is still some years from mastering more sophisticated behaviors. Integrating its subbehaviors so they do not compete is a difficulty that has hardly yet been faced. And Cog has no sense of time. Finding a good way to provide one is a "real challenge," Brooks's team writes in a forthcoming publication. Because the design philosophy requires that Cog function like a human, a digital clock is not acceptable.

Cog's development, it seems, will prove slower than that of a human infant. Perhaps just as well: the team has started to consider the complications that might follow from giving Cog a sense of sexual identity. But the effort to make a machine that acts like a human could yet tell researchers a good deal about how a human acts that way.

PART 2
■ Discussion Questions

1. Cog can locate and fixate on moving objects, can reach and play with stationary objects, and can recognize eyes and faces. By what processes does this robot learn and develop? Are these processes comparable to those that we see in children?

2. What theories of child development do you think guided the programming of this robot?

3. Cog may be thought of as a simulation experiment. However, simulations are only as good as the parameters that are fed into them. Using the article, identify the parameters that were fed into this simulation experiment. Do you think that these parameters are necessary and sufficient to inform us about human developmental processes?

4. Cog has been designed to go through a period of artificial infancy. Given that infants eventually act intentionally, do you think that Cog will eventually be capable of intentional actions?

5. Cog will eventually learn about the properties of its own body and how it can be put in motion. Cog will then learn how to act upon its environment in pursuit of some results. Do you think that by observing Cog's successes and failures through these processes anything of value can be learned about how human infants achieve the same milestones?

Suggested Reading

Adams, B., Breazeal, C., Brooks, R. A., & Scassellati, B. (2000). Humanoid robots: A new kind of tool. *IEEE Intelligent Systems, 15,* 25–31.

Lewin, R. (1994). Birth of a human robot. *New Scientist, 142,* 26–30.

Travis, J. (1994). Building a baby brain in a robot. *Science, 264,* 1080–1082.

For more information on the Cog project and other related artificial intelligence projects visit the MIT Artificial Intelligence Laboratory website: http://www.ai.mit.edu/projects/humanoid-robotics-group

MODULE 9

DESIGNING A BABY TOY

This module allows you to consolidate and utilize knowledge from various aspects of child development. Your task is to divide into small groups and collectively design a new toy appropriate for a particular age group. Pick a target age between 6 months and 18 months. Take full advantage of the child's abilities at that age by considering all aspects of development, such as sensation and perception, motor abilities, and cognitive abilities. Be careful to avoid overestimating the child's abilities and creating a toy too complex for the child to enjoy and appreciate. As a final consideration, be sure to take into account issues of safety and economy.

After conceptualizing your toy, draw a detailed schematic of the toy, and if possible, create a prototype of your new product. Use the following questions as a guideline for presenting and evaluating your toy:

1. What is the name of your toy?
2. For what age is the toy appropriate?
3. What sensory and perceptual abilities does the toy utilize?
4. What degree of fine motor skills is required to maximize the toy's utility?
5. What attention and memory capacities are needed to play with the toy?
6. Is the toy purely for entertainment or does it have educational value?
7. Is the toy durable (will a precocious infant destroy it)? How much should it cost?
8. Does the toy require adult supervision or assistance?
9. Is it safe for a child this age? Is it safe for any younger siblings the child might have?

MODULE 10

BEHAVIORAL INHIBITION

In this module, you will learn about behavioral inhibition, a specific aspect of temperament. Questions are provided for you to use as a tool in assessing whether you were an inhibited child, and to facilitate a discussion of the topic.

INTRODUCTION

Temperament can be defined as *biologically rooted individual differences in behavioral tendencies that are present early in life and are relatively stable across various situations and over time.*

Accordingly, temperament is crucial in a discussion of development, as it is the earliest manifestation of personality; further, it is relevant in predicting the success of a child's adjustment. A child's temperament determines how he or she will respond to various situations, which in turn affects how people will respond to the child. A basic tenet of adjustment is that there must be a good fit between an individual's temperament and the broader social context.

Theorists posit different sets of temperaments, using terms such as activity, mood, and emotionality. Behavioral inhibition is one such term. When a child (or an adult) encounters an unfamiliar person, object, or situation, a state of uncertainty arises. People react to this uncertainty in different ways. Some become quiet, cease activity, seek support, or withdraw. Others show no change, or even approach the uncertainty. We can call the former inhibited and the latter uninhibited. Shyness, fearfulness, or caution are some of the defining characteristics of behavioral inhibition.

Jerome Kagan and his colleagues at Harvard have done extensive work on this aspect of temperament. Part 1 of this module is a reprint of an article describing some of the Harvard group's work on the development of inhibition. Part 2 is a copy of the Retrospective Self-Report of Behavioral Inhibition. Based on your score on this instrument, you can determine whether you might have been like one of the extremely inhibited children in the Kagan studies. Part 3 of the module poses questions about this topic.

PART 1
REQUIRED READING

INITIAL REACTIONS TO UNFAMILIARITY

Jerome Kagan, Nancy Snidman, and Doreen M. Arcus

From Current Directions in Psychological Science, *Vol. 1, No. 6 by J. Kagan, N. Snidman and D. M. Arcus. Copyright © 1992 by Blackwell Publishers. Reprinted by permission.*

All animals regularly encounter events that recruit attention and a vigilant posture because the stimuli share some features with similar events encountered in the past. Some animals typically approach these discrepant events, whereas others typically avoid them. This fact became a fundamental principle for Schneirla,[1] who spent much of his career trying to understand approach-avoidant behavior in animals. There are at least three different questions one can ask about these complementary reactions to unfamiliar events.

One line of inquiry seeks to determine, within or between species, which events consistently elicit approach and which avoidance. The sight of the mother usually provokes the former in mammalian infants; the sight of an unfamiliar adult typically provokes an initial avoidance. A second question asks about interspecific differences in approach or avoidance to the same class of events. One-year-old macaque monkeys avoid, at least initially, an unfamiliar monkey of the same age, whereas 3-year-old children (roughly comparable to 1-year-old monkeys because the macaque grows at a rate three times that of the human) more often approach an unfamiliar peer. Finally, one can ask about intraspecific differences in the tendency to approach or to avoid unfamiliar situations or objects. When the subjects are animals, we talk about strain differences in the reaction to novelty; for example, Maudsley reactive and nonreactive rats and different breeds of dogs respond in different ways to unfamiliar situations.[2] Although humans are not selectively bred for behavior, children differ in their initial propensity to approach or to avoid unfamiliarity. Each of these dispositions is regarded as a temperamental quality as well as one of the Thomas and Chess[3] temperamental dimensions.

A child's environment contains many sources of unfamiliarity, including foods, animals, objects, places, and people, and we apply different adjectives to denote the stimulus basis for the subsequent reactions. Children who avoid eating unfamiliar foods are called finicky; those who avoid unfamiliar animals, objects, or situations are called fearful or timid. If the source of unfamiliarity is a person, we call the avoidant child shy and the one who approaches strangers sociable.

It is important to differentiate, however, between two types of shy children. Some shy children acquire their shy profile primarily as a result of experience alone (e.g., peer or parental rejection).[4] These children are shy with people, but they are less likely to avoid most unfamiliar places and objects. Shy children of the second type are born with a physiology that biases them to acquire an avoidant style to many unfamiliar events—people as well as nonsocial stimulus events. These latter children differ from the former in both autonomic functioning, affect, and physical features[5] and belong to the temperamental category we call *inhibited*. In contrast, children who are born with a physiology that biases them to approach these same unfamiliar events are called *uninhibited*.[6] The physiology is not deterministic, however; both behavioral profiles require actualizing environments.

DEVELOPMENT OF INHIBITED AND UNINHIBITED CHILDREN

It is important to appreciate that the referential meanings of inhibited and uninhibited in our research are based on direct observations of children, rather than parental descriptions derived from interviews or questionnaires. The correlations between parental reports of shy or sociable behavior and behavioral observations that define each of the two categories are positive, but not high, averaging between .2 and .4.

There are many reasons why the relation between the two sources of information is only modest. Parents are not equally discerning in their interpretations of their children's behavior in specific contexts. Further, some parents are subject to contrast effects when they have more than one child and vulnerable to halo effects when they describe their child. More important, one cannot ask parents to evaluate qualities they do not understand completely or to judge characteristics for which there are no familiar English words with consensual meaning. This problem is especially serious when the temperamental constructs refer to behaviors (or physiological reactions) in situations that may not occur in the home environment (e.g., a stranger in a clown costume confronts a child in an unfamiliar room; an unfamiliar woman utters a nonsense phrase in a stern voice; a drop of lemon juice applied to the child's tongue produces a large heart rate acceleration). Developmental psychologists do not rely on parental questionnaires to determine when an infant has attained the object concept or the capacity for cross-modal matching. However, parental questionnaires can be sensitive sources of information for some psychological characteristics; for example, this method appears to be a relatively valid index of a child's expressive vocabulary in the 2nd and 3rd years.

About 15% to 20% of healthy Caucasian children living in stable families typically avoid and become emotionally subdued to unfamiliar situations, people, and objects in the 2nd year of life. A somewhat larger group, about 30% to 35% of the same population, displays the complementary profile of a relatively rapid approach to the same unfamiliar events, often associated with spontaneous vocalization and smiling. Longitudinal study of these two groups revealed that about three quarters of the children who were originally classified as either inhibited or uninhibited in the 2nd year retained their respective behavioral qualities through the 8th year.[5] We presume that many of the children who changed their initial behavioral profiles did so as a result of environmental experiences. For example, one uninhibited child became shy and timid at 4 years of age after her father committed suicide. Children born with either temperamental bias possess the capacity to change their behavior.

The two groups also differ in reactivity of the sympathetic nervous system. For example, inhibited, compared with uninhibited, children display larger magnitudes of heart rate acceleration and pupillary dilation to cognitive stress and show larger rises in diastolic blood pressure when their posture changes from sitting to standing (as a result of a sympathetically mediated vasoconstriction in the arterial tree following a rise to a standing position).[5] Baseline heart rate or blood pressure does not discriminate the groups after 4 months.

The suggestion that these behavioral and physiological differences are influenced by genetic factors is supported by studies of monozygotic and dizygotic twins during the first 3 years of life; the data reveal significant heritabilities for both inhibited and uninhibited behavior (approximately .5).[6]

This corpus of data, combined with related research on animals, suggests that the physiologies that contribute to the two profiles involve, to some degree, the excitability of the amygdala and its projections to the motor system (corpus striatum and central gray), the cingulate and frontal cortex, the hypothalamus, and the sympathetic nervous system.[7]

PREDICTION FROM INFANCY

Although very young infants are neither shy with strangers nor fearful in unfamiliar places, the presumption that the two temperamental types vary in reactivity of several circuits originating in the amygdala provides a clue as to which responses might serve as predictors of inhibited and uninhibited behavior in the 2nd year. The basolateral area of the amygdala, which receives sensory input from the thalamus and cortex, projects to the ventral striatum and ventral pallidum, which, in turn, mediate flexing and extending of arms and legs following stimulation. The central nucleus of the amygdala, which is involved in the emotional states of fear, projects to the cingulate, central gray, hypothalamus, and sympathetic chain. Because these circuits, originating in the amygdala, are associated with motor activity and distress calls in animals, it is reasonable to suggest that variation among young infants in motor reactivity and distress to unfamiliar stimuli might reflect variation in thresholds in these circuits. By providing indices of the two temperamental types, these behaviors might predict later display of inhibited and uninhibited behavior.[8]

Longitudinal study of two independent groups of healthy, 4-month-old Caucasian infants (total N over 400) has revealed that about 20% display extreme degrees of motor activity to moving mobiles, Q-tips dipped in dilute solutions of butyl alcohol, and tape-recorded human voices. These infants extend their arms and legs in momentary spasticity, display bursts of vigorous limb activity, and, on occasion, arch their backs to the presentation of the stimulus events. Further, during some of the periods of vigorous motor activity, these infants fret or cry, suggesting that the distress is a consequence of becoming highly aroused. These infants are called *high reactive*.

A larger group, about 40% of healthy, 4-month-old Caucasian infants, shows the opposite pattern of low motor activity and minimal crying to the same events. These infants occasionally move an arm or a leg, but rarely show spasticity, bursts of limb activity, arching of the back, extreme motor tension, or irritability. They are called *low reactive*. Other infants show either low motor activity with high irritability (about 25% of the population) or high motor activity and minimal distress (about 10% of the population). The remaining infants are difficult to classify because of failure to complete the test battery or inconsistency in their behavior.[9]

When these infants were observed in the laboratory at 14 months as they encountered unfamiliar rooms, people, procedures, and toys, the high-reactive infants were the most fearful, and the low-reactive infants were the least fearful, fear being defined as the occurrence of fretting or crying to an unfamiliar event or procedure (e.g., placement of electrodes or a blood pressure cuff, facial and vocal disapproval from the examiner, a noisy rotating wheel, a request to taste liquid from a dropper) or failure to approach unfamiliar adults or objects despite a friendly invitation to do so. The other two groups showed intermediate levels of fear. Most low-reactive infants in both cohorts showed no fears or one fear (low fear) across a 90-min battery containing 17 episodes, whereas most high-reactive infants had four or more fears (high fear) across the same battery, $F(3, 90) = 7.8$, $p < .001$ for Cohort 1; $F(3, 298) = 30.2$, $p < .0001$ for Cohort 2.

These two profiles were maintained when the same children were observed in a similar battery containing 21 age-appropriate procedures at 21 months of age (see Table 1). Among high-reactive infants, 40% to 50% showed high fear (four or more fears) at both 14 and 21 months, compared with 7% to 10% of the low-reactive infants. By contrast, about 40% of the low-reactive infants showed low fear (no fears or one fear) at both

TABLE 1

PROPORTION OF HIGH- AND LOW-REACTIVE INFANTS DISPLAYING LOW OR HIGH FEAR AT BOTH 14 AND 21 MONTHS OF AGE

Reactivity category	Fear score	
	Low fear (0–1)	High fear (>4)
	Cohort 1 (N = 94)	
High reactive (n = 22)	20	50
Low reactive (n = 31)	45	10
$x^2 = 12.9, p < .01$		
	Cohort 2 (N = 240)	
High reactive (n = 55)	5	40
Low reactive (n = 103)	37	7
$x^2 = 31.4, p < .00001$		

ages, compared with less than 20% of the high-reactive infants. As at 14 months, the two other groups showed intermediate fear scores. However, not all high-reactive 4-month-old infants become inhibited children; the home environment in the 1st year can influence the actualization of the fearful profile.[10]

The high- and low-reactive infants also displayed expected differences in sympathetic reactivity. High-reactive, compared with low-reactive, infants in the first cohort had higher fetal heart rates, higher heart rates at 2 weeks of age during sleep, and larger heart rate accelerations to a sour taste at 14 months of age. Further, high-reactive, high-fear infant girls who showed low levels of smiling were likely to show an asymmetry of temperature on the forehead at 21 months, with the right side cooler than the left by 0.10 °C or more. By contrast, low-reactive, low-fear, high-smiling infant girls were likely to show a cooler left side. The asymmetry in temperature, due to greater cooling on one side, is the result of a sympathetically mediated vasoconstriction of the arterioles mediated by alpha adrenergic receptors. The sympathetic nervous system is a bit more reactive on the right than on the left side of the body; hence, children who cool more on the right than on the left may possess a more reactive sympathetic system.

Davidson and Fox[11] have found that inhibited children display greater desynchronization of alpha activity in the right frontal area (i.e., greater activation), and uninhibited children show greater desynchronization in the left frontal area. These results are in accord with the asymmetries in facial cooling and with a growing literature suggesting that the right hemisphere participates more fully than the left in the mediation of dysphoric affect.

We believe, but have not yet proven, that inhibited and uninhibited children, who are extreme in their behavior, belong to qualitatively different categories, even though the actual measurements of fearfulness, shyness, and sociability form continuous distributions in large unselected samples—a point of view supported by other scientists.[12] The empirical bases for this claim are the different profiles of physical features (e.g., eye color, width of face) and physiology displayed by the two behavioral groups. It is likely that inhibited and uninhibited children represent only two of a potentially large number of temperamental categories that will be discovered in the future. Each category will be characterized at each developmental stage by a distinct behavioral and biological profile that emerges from the joint influence of a particular physiology and environmental encounters that either strengthen or weaken the tendencies that are inherently prepotent for each group.

Acknowledgments—This research was supported in part by grants from the John D. and Catherine T. MacArthur Foundation and the Leon Lowenstein Foundation.

Notes

1. T. C. Schneirla, Aspects of stimulation and organization in approach-withdrawal processes underlying vertebrate development, in *Advances in the Study of Behavior*. D. S. Lehrman, R. A. Hinde, and E. P. Shaw, Eds. (Academic Press, New York, 1965).
2. P. I. Broadhurst, The Maudsley reactive and non-reactive strains of rats, *Behavior Genetics*, 5, 299–319 (1975); M. E. Goddard and R. G. Beilharz, A multi-variate analysis of the genetics of fearfulness in potential guide dogs, *Behavior Genetics*, 15, 69–89 (1985).
3. A. Thomas and S. Chess, *Temperament and Development* (Brunner Mazel, New York, 1977).
4. M. Putallaz, Maternal behavior and children's sociometric status, *Child Development*, 58, 324–370 (1987).
5. J. Kagan, J. S. Reznick, and N. Snidman, Biological bases of childhood shyness, *Science*, 240, 167–173 (1988).
6. A. P. Matheny, Children's behavioral inhibition over age and across situations, *Journal of Personality*, 37, 215–235 (1989), R. Plomin. J. Campos, R. Corley, R. N. Emde, D. Fulker, J. Kagan, J. S. Reznick, J. Robinson, C. Zahn-Waxler, and J. C. DeFries, Individual differences during the second year of life: The MacArthur Longitudinal Twin Study, in *Individual Differences in Infancy*, J. Colombo and J. Fagen, Eds. (Erlbaum, Hillsdale, NJ, 1990).
7. L. T. Dunn and B. J. Everitt, Double dissociations of the effects of amygdala and insular cortex lesions on conditioned taste aversion, passive avoidance, and neophobia in the rat using the excitotoxin ibotenic acid. *Behavioral Neuroscience*, 102, 3–19 (1988); A. E. Kelley, V. B. Domesick, and W. J. H. Nauta, The amygdalostriatal projection in the rat, *Neuroscience*, 7, 615–630 (1982).
8. M. Mishkin and J. Aggleton, Multiple functional contributions of the amygdala in the monkey, in *The Amygdala Complex*, Y. Ben-Ari, Ed., INSERM Symposium No. 20 (North-Holland Biomedical Press, Amsterdam, 1981).
9. J. Kagan and N. Snidman, Infant predictors of inhibited and uninhibited profiles, *Psychological Science*, 2, 40–44 (1991): J. Kagan and N. Snidman, Temperamental factors in human development. *American Psychologist*, 46, 856–862 (1991).
10. D. M. Arcus, *The experiential modification of temperamental bias in inhibited and uninhibited children,* unpublished doctoral dissertation. Harvard University, Cambridge, MA (1991).

11. R. J. Davidson, Emotion and affective style: Hemispheric substrates, *Psychological Science, 1*, 39–43 (1992); N. A. Fox, If it's not left, it's right. *American Psychologist, 46*, 863–872 (1991).
12. A. S. Clarke, W. A. Mason, and G. P. Moberg, Differential behavioral and adrenocortical responses to stress among three macaque species. *American Journal of Primatology, 14*, 37–52 (1988); J. P. Scott and J. L. Fuller, *Genetics and the Social Behavior of the Dog* (University of Chicago Press, Chicago, 1965); D. Magnusson, *Individual Development From an Interactional Perspective: A Longitudinal Study* (Erlbaum, Hillsdale, NJ, 1988); R. A. Hinde and A. Dennis, Categorizing individuals, *International Journal of Behavioral Development*, 105–119 (1986).

Recommended Reading

Kagan, J. (1989). The concept of behavioral inhibition to the unfamiliar. In *Perspectives on Behavioral Inhibition*, J. S. Reznick, Ed. (University of Chicago Press, Chicago).

Rothbart, M. K. (1989). Temperament in childhood: A framework. In *Temperament in Childhood*, G. A. Kohnstamm, J. E. Bates, and M. K. Rothbart, Eds. (Wiley, New York).

PART 2

■ Retrospective Self-Report of Inhibition—Version 2.0

© J. Steven Reznick, UNC—Chapel Hill, CB#3270, Chapel Hill, NC 27599-3270

The following questions are about things you may have done and feelings you may have had as a child. In answering these questions, please think of yourself as you were in elementary school (grades 1–6). If you cannot remember, or are not sure about an answer, please make your best guess.

Please circle the appropriate answer:

1. On average, how often per year were you absent from school due to illness?
   1. 0–4 days   2. 5–9 days   3. 10–14 days   4. 15–19 days   5. 20 or more days
2. On average, how often per year were you sent to the nurse's office due to illness?
   1. 0–4 days   2. 5–9 days   3. 10–14 days   4. 15–19 days   5. 20 or more days
3. Did you have illnesses/symptoms such as headaches or stomachaches for which the doctors could not find a cause?
   1. never   2. rarely   3. sometimes   4. often   5. very often
4. How often did you have nightmares?
   1. never   2. once a year   3. once a month   4. once a week   5. once a night
5. Were you scared of the dark?
   1. never   2. rarely   3. sometimes   4. often   5. always
6. Was it necessary for you or your parents to check under your bed or in your closet before you went to sleep?
   1. never   2. rarely   3. sometimes   4. often   5. always
7. Did you need to have a special stuffed animal, blanket, or toy with you so that you could fall asleep?
   1. never   2. rarely   3. sometimes   4. often   5. always

8. Were you afraid of dogs, cats, or other domestic animals?
   1. never   2. rarely   3. sometimes   4. often   5. always
9. Were you afraid of unfamiliar animals, such as those you encountered on the street or at someone else's home?
   1. never   2. rarely   3. sometimes   4. often   5. always
10. Were you scared that you would be kidnapped or otherwise separated from your parents?
    1. never   2. rarely   3. sometimes   4. often   5. very often
11. Did it upset you when your parents left you with a new, unfamiliar baby-sitter?
    1. never   2. rarely   3. sometimes   4. often   5. always
12. When your parents went out without you, were you scared that they might not come back?
    1. never   2. rarely   3. sometimes   4. often   5. always
13. Did you sleep over at friends' houses?
    1. very often   2. often   3. sometimes   4. rarely   5. never
14. Did you try new foods?
    1. eagerly   2. agreeably   3. with coaxing   4. only if pressured   5. never
15. Were you usually scared on the first day of a new school year?
    1. not at all   2. slightly   3. moderately   4. very   5. terrified
16. Did you ever pretend to be sick in order to avoid going to school or to social events?
    1. never   2. rarely   3. sometimes   4. often   5. very often
17. Did it upset you to be called up to the blackboard?
    1. not at all   2. slightly   3. moderately   4. very   5. extremely
18. Did it upset you to be called on, even if you knew the answer?
    1. not at all   2. slightly   3. moderately   4. very   5. extremely
19. Did your teachers have trouble hearing you when you spoke or answered a question in class?
    1. never   2. rarely   3. sometimes   4. often   5. always
20. If there was something that you did not understand in class, did you ask the teacher for help?
    1. always   2. often   3. sometimes   4. rarely   5. never
21. During recess, did you play with the main group of children?
    1. always   2. often   3. sometimes   4. rarely   5. never
22. Did you enjoy participating in party games?
    1. always   2. often   3. sometimes   4. rarely   5. never
23. Did you enjoy meeting new children your age?
    1. always   2. often   3. sometimes   4. rarely   5. never
24. Did your voice squeak, crack, or sound shaky when you were talking in front of a group of people?
    1. never   2. rarely   3. sometimes   4. often   5. always
25. How popular did you feel?
    1. very   2. moderately   3. average   4. below average   5. not at all

26. Did you have any problems with, or have to see a doctor for allergies, sleeplessness, or constipation?

   1. never 2. rarely 3. sometimes 4. often 5. very often

27. Did you need a night-light or hall light on in order to go to sleep?

   1. never 2. rarely 3. sometimes 4. often 5. always

28. Did you willingly participate in group singing or plays?

   1. always 2. often 3. sometimes 4. rarely 5. never

29. Were your feelings easily hurt?

   1. never 2. rarely 3. sometimes 4. often 5. very often

30. Did you tell your friends or family members when you were angry with them?

   1. always 2. often 3. sometimes 4. rarely 5. never

To score these questions, add the circled numbers across the 30 questions (e.g., an answer of "0–4 days" on question 1 is worth 1 point; an answer of "20 or more days" is worth 5 points). If you left an item blank, count it as 3 points.

Based on scores from college-aged students at other schools, the expected mean score should be 67. Higher scores indicate more inhibition, with scores above 81–82 reflecting the upper 10% or extreme inhibition. Scores below 54–55 reflect the extreme lack of inhibition.

PART 3
Discussion Questions

1. Natural selection seems to reward both inhibition and the lack of inhibition (that is, both types of individual are prevalent). What would be the consequences if too many people were either extremely inhibited or uninhibited?

2. Think of examples of people you know who have become more inhibited due to some sort of experience. What happened? Was the effect short-term or long-term? Is the person's age at the time of the experience relevant for understanding the effect?

3. How might different contexts be expected to influence children to become more or less inhibited? For example, what direction of change would be encouraged in the classroom? What direction of change would be encouraged at summer camp? Think of examples of practices in various cultures that might encourage or discourage inhibition.

4. On the basis of what you have read about inhibition and about children in general, think of procedures that could be used to determine the relative degree of inhibition among first graders.

5. Given that extreme inhibition often has strong biological support, what sort of advice would you give to a parent who has an extremely inhibited child? Would you recommend training and experiences that attempt to change the child or would you recommend acceptance, support, and strategies to help the child cope with his or her shyness?

■ SUGGESTED READING

Kagan, J. (1994). *Galen's Prophecy*. Basic Books: New York, NY.

Kagan, J., Reznick, J. S., & Snidman, N. (1988). Biological bases of childhood shyness. *Science, 240*, 167–171.

MODULE 11

ATTACHMENT THEORY AS EXPLAINED BY ITS AUTHORS

Attachment theory is based primarily on the work of John Bowlby (1907–1991) and Mary Salter Ainsworth (1913–1999). In this module you will learn about the origins of attachment theory by reading an article published by Ainsworth and Bowlby that provides a historical account of their separate and joint contributions to attachment theory.

INTRODUCTION

Attachment refers to the enduring emotional tie between a child and her caregiver. John Bowlby formulated much of the conceptual foundation of attachment theory. He believed that human infants are born with a set of built-in attachment behaviors, such as clinging, following, crying, and smiling, whose function is to keep the caregiver nearby. Over evolutionary time, these attachment behaviors were selected because this proximity protected the infant from predators and increased the probability that its biological needs would be met. Bowlby proposed that the quality of the attachment bond is influenced by the caregiver's sensitivity to the infant's signals and needs. Over time, the quality of the adult responses determines the kinds of beliefs or expectations the infant develops about herself and about others. The set of these beliefs is called an *internal working model.* According to Bowlby, the formation of this internal working model is the mechanism by which the quality of attachment influences future behavior.

The *strange situation* procedure, developed by Mary Ainsworth, is designed to provide a set of criteria to evaluate the quality of the infant's attachment to her caregiver. This procedure is typically used with 12- to 18-month-olds, and consists of eight episodes in which the mother and a female stranger interact with, depart from and reunite with the infant in a laboratory playroom. Based on observations of the infant's patterns of exploration in the presence and absence of the caregiver, expressions of distress, and greeting behaviors during reunion episodes, Ainsworth has offered well-defined criteria to classify infants as securely attached, insecure-avoidant, and insecure-ambivalent/resistant. The possibility to measure attachment security using Ainsworth's Strange Situation procedure contributed importantly to the wide acceptance of Bowlby's theoretical framework in developmental psychology.

PART 1
REQUIRED READING

AN ETHOLOGICAL APPROACH TO PERSONALITY DEVELOPMENT

Mary D. Salter Ainsworth, *University of Virginia*
John Bowlby, *Tavistock Clinic, London, England*

From American Psychologist, *Vol. 46, No. 4 by Mary D. Ainsworth and John Bowlby. Copyright © 1991 by the American Psychological Association. Reprinted with permission.*

This is a historical account of the partnership in which Bowlby and Ainsworth participated to develop attachment theory and research. Beginning with their separate approaches to understanding personality development before Ainsworth joined Bowlby's research team at the Tavistock Clinic in London for 4 years, it describes the origins of the ethological approach that they adopted. After Ainsworth left London, her research in Uganda and in Baltimore lent empirical support to Bowlby's theoretical constructions. The article shows how their contributions to attachment theory and research interdigitated in a partnership that endured for 40 years across time and distance.

The distinguishing characteristic of the theory of attachment that we have jointly developed is that it is an ethological approach to personality development. We have had a long and happy partnership in pursuing this approach. In this article we wish to give a brief historical account of the initially separate but compatible approaches that eventually merged in the partnership, and how our contributions have intertwined in the course of developing an ethologically oriented theory of attachment and a body of research that has both stemmed from the theory and served to extend and elaborate it.

BEFORE 1950

Even before beginning graduate training, each of us became keenly interested in personality development and the key role played in it by the early interaction between children and parents. In Bowlby's case this was kindled by volunteer work in a residential school for maladjusted children, which followed his undergraduate studies in medicine at Cambridge University. Two children especially impressed him. One was an isolated, affectionless adolescent who had never experienced a stable relationship with a mother figure, and the other was an anxious child who followed Bowlby around like a shadow. Largely because of these two children, Bowlby resolved to continue his medical studies toward a specialty in child psychiatry and psychotherapy, and was accepted as a student for psychoanalytic training. From early in his training he believed that analysts, in their preoccupation with a child's fantasy life, were paying too little attention to actual events in the child's real life. His experience at the London Child Guidance Clinic convinced him of the significant role played by interaction with parents in the development of a child's personality, and of the ways in which this interaction had been influenced by a parent's early experiences with his or her own parents. His first systematic research was begun also at the London Child Guidance Clinic, where he compared 44 juvenile thieves with a matched control group and found that prolonged experiences of mother–child separation or deprivation of maternal care were much more common among the thieves than in the control group, and that such experiences were especially linked to children diagnosed as affectionless (Bowlby, 1944).

The outbreak of war in 1939 interrupted Bowlby's career as a child psychiatrist but brought him useful research experience in connection with officer selection and with a new group of congenial associates, some of whom at the end of the war joined together to reorganize the Tavistock Clinic. Soon afterward the clinic became part of the National Health Service, and Bowlby served as full-time consultant psychiatrist and director of the Department for Children and Parents. There he also picked up the threads of his clinical and research interests.

Unfortunately, the Kleinian orientation of several members of the staff made it difficult to use clinic cases for the kind of research Bowlby wanted to undertake. He established a research unit of his own, which began operations in 1948. Convinced of the significance of real-life events on the course of child development, he chose to focus on the effects of early separation from the mother because separation was an event on record, unlike disturbed family interaction, of which, in those days, there were no adequate records.

Members of the research team began two research projects, one retrospective, the other prospective. The retrospective project was a follow-up study of 66 school-age children who had experienced separation from their families in a tuberculosis sanatorium at some time between the ages of one and four years, and who had subsequently returned home. The prospective project was undertaken single-handedly by James Robertson, then a social worker, who had had experience in Anna Freud's wartime nursery. Robertson observed young children's behavior as they underwent separation in three different institutional settings. Where possible, he observed the children's behavior in interaction with parents at home, both prior to the separation and after they were reunited with them. Bowlby himself undertook a third project, in response to a request by the World Health Organization (WHO) to prepare a report on what was known of the fate of children without families. This request led him to read all the available literature on separation and maternal deprivation, and to travel widely to find out what was being done elsewhere about the care of motherless children. The report was published both by WHO as a monograph entitled *Maternal Care and Mental Health* (Bowlby, 1951) and subsequently in a popular Penguin edition with the title *Child Care and the Growth of Love* (Bowlby & Ainsworth, 1965).

Let us turn now to the beginnings of Ainsworth's career. She entered the honor course in psychology as an undergraduate at the University of Toronto, hoping (as many do) to understand how she had come to be the person she was, and what her parents had to do with it. She was interested in the whole wide range of courses available to her, but in two particularly. One was run as a class experiment by S. N. F. Chant, in which she learned that research is a fascinating pursuit. The other, taught by William E. Blatz, focused on Blatz's newly formulated theory of security as an approach to understanding personality development. After graduation Ainsworth continued on at the University of Toronto as a graduate student, and was delighted when Blatz proposed that she base her dissertation research on his security theory.

Because she carried some highlights of security theory with her into attachment theory, it is appropriate here to say something about it (Blatz, 1966).[1] *Security*, as its Latin root—*sine cura*—would suggest, means "without care" or "without anxiety." According to Blatz, there are several kinds of security, of which the first to develop is what he called *immature dependent security*. Infants, and to a decreasing extent young children, can feel secure only if they can rely on parent figures to take care of them and take responsibility for the consequences of their behavior. Children's appetite for change leads them to be curious about the world

---

[1] Blatz's security theory was largely embedded in an oral tradition, from which those who listened drew different meanings. Ainsworth has dwelt on those aspects that particularly influenced her at the time. Blatz's own 1966 account contained much that is at variance with what Ainsworth carried into attachment theory.

around them and to explore it and learn about it. But learning itself involves insecurity. If and when children become uneasy or frightened while exploring, they are nevertheless secure if they can retreat to a parent figure, confident that they will receive comfort and reassurance. Thus the parent's availability provides the child with a secure base from which to explore and learn.

As children gradually gain knowledge about the world and learn skills to cope with it, they can increasingly rely on themselves and thus acquire a gradually increasing basis for *independent security*. By the time of reaching maturity, according to Blatz, a person should be fully emancipated from parents. Blatz viewed any substantial continuation of dependence on them to be undesirable. But one cannot be secure solely on the basis of one's independent knowledge and skills. To be secure, a person needs to supplement with *mature dependent security* whatever degree of independent security he or she has managed to achieve. Blatz thought of this as occurring in a mutually contributing, give-and-take relationship with another of one's own generation—a relationship in which each partner, on the basis of his or her knowledge and skills, can provide a secure base to the other. Blatz also acknowledged that defense mechanisms (he called them *deputy agents*) could provide a temporary kind of security, but did not themselves deal with the source of the insecurity—like treating a toothache with an analgesic.

For her dissertation, Ainsworth (then Salter, 1940) constructed two self-report, paper-pencil scales intended to assess the degree to which a person was secure rather than insecure. The first scale concerned relations with parents, and the second relations with friends. Together these scales were intended to indicate the extent to which the person's security rested on immature dependence on parents, independence, mature dependent relations with age peers, or the pseudosecurity of defense mechanisms. Individual differences were identified in terms of patterns of scores—a classificatory type of assessment for which she found much later use. The subjects were third-year university students, for each of whom an autobiography was available as a validity check.

To anticipate her later evaluation in the light of further experience, Ainsworth came to believe that Blatz's security theory did not deal adequately with defensive processes. Rejecting Freud's theory of unconscious processes, Blatz held that only conscious processes were of any significance in personality development. This was one aspect of his theory that Ainsworth did not carry forward. Furthermore, it became clear to her that with the self-report paper-pencil method of appraisal it is well-nigh impossible to assess accurately how much defensive maneuvers have inflated security scores. However, the general trends in her dissertation findings gave support to security theory as formulated at the time, and sustained her enthusiasm for it.

Upon completing her degree in 1939, Ainsworth hoped to continue security research with Blatz, and sought and obtained an appointment to the faculty. Their research plan was interrupted by the outbreak of war three months later. Blatz and most of the other faculty of the department soon departed for war-related jobs. Ainsworth continued teaching until 1942, but then joined the newly established Canadian Women's Army Corps, where she was assigned to personnel selection. After V-E Day, she spent a year as Superintendent of Women's Rehabilitation in the Department of Veterans' Affairs. In 1946 she happily returned to the University of Toronto as an assistant professor of psychology.

Through her war work she had developed an interest in clinical assessment, and she chose this as her area of academic specialization. She focused on projective techniques, especially the Rorschach, which she learned through workshops directed by Bruno Klopfer. This led to coauthorship of a book on the Rorschach technique (Klopfer, Ainsworth, Klopfer, & Holt, 1954). She gained practical experience in clinical assessment as a volunteer in a veterans' hospital, and as planned earlier, she codirected research with Blatz into further assessments of security.

In 1950 she left the University of Toronto, having married Leonard Ainsworth, a member of the security research team who had been admitted for PhD training at the University of London. Jobless, she was guided by Edith Mercer, a friend she had met during the war years, to an advertisement in the *Times Educational Supplement*. This sought a developmental researcher, proficient in projective techniques, for a project at the

Tavistock Clinic investigating the effect on personality development of separation from the mother in early childhood. She got the job—and it transformed her research career, while at the same time incorporating some of its earlier threads.

1950 TO 1954

Bowlby had just completed his report for the WHO when Ainsworth joined his research team. She was put to work reading the literature he had incorporated into the report and, like Bowlby, was impressed by the evidence of the adverse effects on development attributable to the lack of interaction with a mother figure when infants and young children spent prolonged periods in impersonal institutional care. She also joined in the team's analysis of the data yielded by the other two projects. It was clear that the richer yield came from the prospective study. Direct observation in the child's real-life environment showed how a young child passed from initial distressed protest upon being separated from his mother, to despair, and then finally to detachment, especially if the separation exceeded a week or so. Upon reunion it was clear that the child's tie to its mother had not disappeared, but that it had become anxious. In cases in which detachment lasted beyond separation and initial reunion a continuation of the bond could be inferred, even though it was masked by defensive processes (Bowlby, 1953; Robertson & Bowlby, 1952). A classificatory analysis of the social worker's interviews of the sanatorium follow-up cases confirmed that persistent insecurity of child–mother attachment endured for some years after long, institutional separation, with very few having regained a secure attachment—but indeed few having continued in a condition of affectionless detachment (Bowlby, Ainsworth, Boston, & Rosenbluth, 1956).

During this period Jimmy Robertson (1952) made his film *A Two-Year-Old Goes to Hospital,* as an illustration of the distress caused even by a short separation of several days. This film had immediate impact and Jimmy increasingly turned from research activities toward impressing the public with the urgent need for improvements in the way that young children were cared for while separated from their families. Although Bowlby strongly supported the reforms that followed Jimmy's efforts, he refused to be drawn away from an emphasis on research and theory. He and Ainsworth were both concerned with the multiplicity of the variables that influence the effect of separation, and published a monograph discussing how they need to be considered in planning strategies in separation research (Ainsworth & Bowlby, 1953).

Bowlby, meanwhile, had begun a search for an adequate explanation of the empirical findings, having found none in current psychoanalytic theories to account for young children's responses to separation and reunion, or indeed how the tie to the mother develops. At this point Konrad Lorenz's work on imprinting became available in translation. Sensing its possible relevance to his problem and encouraged by Julian Huxley, Bowlby began delving into the ethological literature. He found the descriptions of separation distress and proximity seeking of precocial birds, who had become imprinted on the mother, strikingly similar to those of young children. He was also struck by the evidence that a strong social bond can be formed that is not based on oral gratification. Furthermore he was impressed with the fact that ethological research began with field observations of the animal in its natural environment, a starting point analogous to that of a clinician. His ethological reading led him to evolutionary biology, and also to systems theory.

During the early 1950s Bowlby was also deeply influenced by his membership in an international and interdisciplinary study group on the psychobiology of the child convened by the World Health Organization, which met annually. Among the members were Piaget, Lorenz, and Margaret Mead, and among guest speakers were Julian Huxley, von Bertalanffy, and Erik Erikson. Bowlby reported on these meetings and the plethora of new ideas he was entertaining at meetings of the research team, but no one took time then to dig into these fields themselves.

In the autumn of 1953 Ainsworth's time at the Tavistock Clinic was drawing to a close, her husband having completed his doctoral work. She had become fascinated with the issues Bowlby's research team had been exploring. She resolved that wherever she went next she would undertake research into what goes on between an infant and its mother that accounts for the formation of its strong bond to her, and the absence or the interruption of which can have such an adverse effect on personality development. She also resolved to base her study on direct observations of infants and mothers in the context of home and family. The first opportunity came at the East African Institute of Social Research in Kampala, Uganda, where her husband obtained a research appointment beginning early in 1954.

Her link with Bowlby and his research team continued for a while after arriving in Kampala. In particular, she remembers a document that he circulated that resulted from his theoretical explorations and foreshadowed a series of publications of his new ethologically based theory of attachment. She read it with great interest, but suggested that his new theory needed to be tested empirically. And, in effect, that is what she has spent the rest of her research career attempting to provide—beginning with a project observing Ganda babies and their mothers in their village homes, with the support of the East African Institute of Social Research.

1954 TO 1963

Meanwhile, Bowlby continued his theory-oriented explorations of the relevant literature in ethology, evolution theory, systems theory, and cognitive psychology, as well as rereading psychoanalytic literature pertinent to his theme. His guide to ethology was Robert Hinde, who began to attend seminars at the Tavistock Institute in 1954. They had a profound influence on each other. Bowlby was drawn further into the animal research literature, notably including Harlow's work with infant monkeys, which supported his conviction that it is proximity to and close bodily contact with a mother figure that cements the infant's attachment rather than the provision of food. On the other hand, the connection with Bowlby led Hinde to study both the interaction of infant rhesus monkeys with their mothers and the effects of mother–infant separation; his findings lent experimental support to Bowlby's position. Although much influenced by the ethologists' observations of other species, Bowlby remained a clinician, continuing to see children and families and to practice individual and family psychotherapy. Moreover, for 20 years he ran a mother's group in a well-baby clinic, learning much from his informal observations of mother–child interaction there, and from the reports of mothers about their children's behavior.

Several classic papers emerged from this theoretical ferment, in each of which his new ethological approach was contrasted with then current psychoanalytic theories: first, "The Nature of the Child's Tie to His Mother" (Bowlby, 1958), then in rapid succession two papers on separation anxiety (Bowlby, 1960b, 1961b), and three on grief and mourning (Bowlby, 1960a, 1961a, 1963). In the first paper he proposed that a baby's attachment came about through a repertoire of genetically based behaviors that matured at various times from birth to several months of age, and became focused on the principal caregiver, usually the mother. This repertoire included crying, sucking, smiling, clinging, and following—of which he considered the latter two the most central. He also discussed how these behaviors were activated and terminated, at first independently before an attachment was formed, but afterward as organized together toward the attachment figure. Finally, he emphasized the active nature of attachment behavior, contrasting it with the passive conception of dependence. Whereas in traditional theory dependence is considered inevitable in infancy, regressive and undesirable in later years, and having no biological value, he conceived of attachment behavior as a major component of human behavioral equipment, on a par with eating and sexual behavior, and as having protection as its biological function, not only in childhood but throughout life. Its presence in humans, as in many other species, could be understood in terms of evolution theory.

The papers on separation anxiety were based partly on research by a new member of the team, Christoph Heinicke (e.g., Heinicke, 1956; Heinicke & Westheimer, 1966), but chiefly on Robertson's observations, which were discussed earlier. Bowlby reviewed six psychoanalytic explanations of separation anxiety, but rejected them in favor of his own hypothesis. He believed that separation anxiety occurs when attachment behavior is activated by the absence of the attachment figure, but cannot be terminated. It differs from fright, which is aroused by some alarming or noxious feature of the environment and activates escape responses. However, fright also activates attachment behavior, so that the baby not only tries to escape from the frightening stimulus but also tries to reach a haven of safety—the attachment figure. Later in infancy, the baby is capable of expectant anxiety in situations that seem likely to be noxious or in which the attachment figure is likely to become unavailable. He emphasized that only a specific figure, usually the mother figure, could terminate attachment behavior completely once it had been intensely activated. He went on to point out that hostility toward the mother is likely to occur when attachment behavior is frustrated, as it is when the child is separated from her, rejected by her, or when she gives major attention to someone else. When such circumstances are frequent or prolonged, primitive defensive processes may be activated, with the result that the child may appear to be indifferent to its mother (as in the detachment attributable to separation) or may be erroneously viewed as healthily independent.

Whereas separation anxiety dominates the protest phase of response to separation, with its heightened but frustrated attachment behavior mingled with anger, grief and mourning dominate the despair phase, as the frustration of separation is prolonged. Bowlby disagreed with the psychoanalytic theorists who held that infants and young children are incapable of mourning and experiencing grief, and also with those who, like Melanie Klein, believed that the loss of the breast at weaning is the greatest loss in infancy. In his papers on grief and mourning he pointed to the similarities between adults and young children in their responses to loss of a loved one: thoughts and behavior expressing longing for the loved one, hostility, appeals for help, despair, and finally reorganization. Many fellow psychoanalysts have vigorously rejected his views on grief and mourning, as indeed they have protested his ethological approach to the child's tie to the mother and his interpretation of separation anxiety. Having been trained in another theoretical paradigm, they have found it difficult to break out of it enough to entertain a new way of viewing old problems.

Meanwhile, in Uganda, Ainsworth had begun her study of Ganda babies. She assembled a sample of 28 unweaned babies and their mothers from several villages near Kampala and, with a splendid interpreter-assistant, visited their homes every two weeks over a period of nine months. They interviewed the mother about her infant-care practices and about the infant's development, and observed their behavior in interaction, and that of the rest of the household. What she saw did not support the Freudian notion of a passive, recipient, narcissistic infant in the oral phase. Rather, she was impressed by the babies' active search for contact with the mother when they were alarmed or hurt, when she moved away or left even briefly, and when they were hungry—and even then she was struck by their initiative in seeking the breast and managing the feeding. There was impressive evidence of the use of the mother as a secure base from which to explore the world and as a haven of safety. She observed the very beginnings of the infant's formation of attachment to the mother in differential termination of crying, and differential smiling and vocalization. Indications that an attachment had clearly been formed were distress and following when separation occurred or threatened, and forms of greeting when mother returned from an absence.

She divided the babies into three groups: securely attached, insecurely attached, and nonattached. Insecurely attached babies cried a lot even when the mother was present, whereas securely attached babies cried little unless mothers were absent or seemed about to leave. Nonattached babies were left alone for long periods by unresponsive mothers but, because they were the youngest in the sample, Ainsworth now believes that they may merely have been delayed in developing attachment. She devised several rather crude scales for rating maternal behavior, of which three significantly differentiated the mothers of secure babies from the others. In retrospect she sees how all three reflected some facet of mother's accessibility and responsiveness to infant behavioral signals. At the time she was pleased that her data meshed with what she had learned about Bowlby's new attachment theory, and also with aspects of Blatz's security theory. However, it was not for some years, after having both begun a second longitudinal study and followed later developments of Bowlby's attachment theory, that the full findings of the Ganda study were published (Ainsworth, 1967).

The Ainsworths left Uganda late in the summer of 1955 and went to Baltimore, where Leonard had found a position. Early in 1956, Mary asked Wendell Garner, then chairman of the Department of Psychology at Johns Hopkins University, about job possibilities in Baltimore. To her surprise and delight he patched together a job for her there as a clinical psychologist, although there was no official vacancy in the department. She was expected to teach the scheduled courses on personality and assessment in this experimental department, and to give to interested students a taste of clinical experience at the Sheppard and Enoch Pratt Hospital, where a part-time appointment for her had been arranged. To supplement her low salary, she began a part-time private practice in diagnostic assessment, mostly with children, aided enormously by her research experience at the Tavistock Clinic.

Ainsworth's desire to begin another longitudinal study of the development of attachment had to be put on hold, but her subsequent work greatly benefited from the clinical experience she obtained meanwhile. She did, however, publish some review papers on maternal deprivation and separation (e.g., Ainsworth, 1962), coauthor with her husband a book on security measurement (Ainsworth & Ainsworth, 1958), and begin work on the data collected in Uganda. In the spring of 1959 John Bowlby visited Baltimore, and she had an opportunity to fill him in on the details of what she was finding in the Ganda data. This served to revive their association, which had lapsed somewhat, and he included her in the Tavistock Mother–Infant Interaction Study Group that had just begun to meet biennially. At the second meeting she gave a preliminary report of her Ganda study (Ainsworth, 1963). The meetings of this interdisciplinary, international group reignited her eagerness to pursue developmental research, and provided a stimulating scientific support network. In 1961 she sought successfully to be released from her clinical role at Johns Hopkins, and to focus on developmental research and teaching. In 1962 she obtained a grant to begin the second longitudinal study that she had so long wanted to do, and in 1963 she was promoted to full professor with tenure.

1963 TO 1980

Having hired Barbara Wittig as a research assistant, Ainsworth located a sample of 15 infant–mother pairs through pediatricians in private practice, usually before the baby's birth. Data collection proceeded during 1963 and 1964. Visits were made to the families every 3 weeks from 3 to 54 weeks after the baby's birth. Each visit lasted for approximately 4 hours, resulting in about 72 hours of observation altogether for each dyad. In 1966–1967, with two new assistants (Robert Marvin and George Allyn), 11 more dyads were added to the sample. Direct observation of behavior was supplemented by information yielded in informal conversations with the mother. Notes made during the visit were later dictated in a narrative account, and then transcribed; these raw data took up two full drawers in a filing cabinet. (Needless to say the data took years to analyze, even with the help of many valued research associates and student assistants.)

The home visitor had been alerted to note infant behaviors that had been earlier identified as attachment behaviors by both Bowlby and Ainsworth, and to pay particular attention to situations in which they were most likely to occur, and to the mother's response to them. Data reduction procedures included event coding, rating, and classification. The data analysis yielded information about both normative development and how individual differences in the security or insecurity of the infants' attachment to their mothers were related to the mothers' behavior.

At the end of the baby's first year, baby and mother were introduced to a 20-minute laboratory situation—the strange situation—a preliminary report of which was made by Ainsworth and Wittig (1969). Although this situation was originally designed for a normative exploration, it turned out to provide a relatively quick method of assessment of infant–mother attachment. This procedure soon became widely used, if not always wisely and well, and has quite overshadowed the findings of the research project that gave rise to it and on which its validity depended. However, the longitudinal home visit data, (which include information about how mother's behavior is linked to the course of infant development) and the strange situation together have yielded important information about the development of attachment in infancy.

The findings of the data analyses of both the strange situation and the home visits were published in a series of articles beginning in 1969 as each analysis was completed. The original research reports were coauthored by the research associate or assistant who was chiefly involved in each piece of data analysis. Ainsworth is deeply indebted to their dedicated and creative contributions.

Highlights of the findings are as follows. Mothers who fairly consistently responded promptly to infant crying early-on had infants who by the end of the first year cried relatively little and were securely attached. Indeed, mothers who were sensitively and appropriately responsive to infant signals in general, including feeding signals, fostered secure infant–mother attachment (Ainsworth & Bell, 1969; Ainsworth, Blehar, Waters, & Wall, 1978; Bell & Ainsworth, 1972). As Bowlby implied from the beginning, close bodily contact with the mother terminates attachment behavior that has been intensely activated. Full-blown crying indicates such intense activation, and indeed our mothers' most usual response to such crying was to pick the baby up (Bell & Ainsworth, 1972). It was not the total amount of time that the baby was held by the mother that promoted secure attachment so much as the contingency of the pick-up with infant signals of desire for contact, and the manner in which the mother then held and handled the baby. Babies who were securely attached not only responded positively to being picked up, being readily comforted if they had been upset, but also they responded positively to being put down, and were likely to turn toward exploration. Timely and appropriate close bodily contact does not "spoil" babies, making them fussy and clingy (Ainsworth, 1979).

About the middle of the first year the babies had clearly become attached, and one of the signs of this was that they began to show distress when mother left the room (separation anxiety). However, babies whose attachment was secure seemed to build up a working model of mother as being available even though out of sight, and thus came to protest little everyday departures at home less often than did infants who were insecurely attached. On the other hand, they were more likely than insecure babies to greet the mother positively upon reunion, and less likely to greet her grumpily or with a cry (Stayton & Ainsworth, 1973; Stayton, Ainsworth, & Main, 1973). However, if the mother left when the baby was mildly stressed by an unfamiliar situation, as in the strange situation, even a secure child was likely to protest her departure. A useful paradox that emerged was that some infants who were clearly insecure at home, showing frequent separation protest or crying a lot in general, were apparently indifferent to their mothers' departure in the strange situation and avoided them upon reunion. Our interpretation was that under the increased stress of the unfamiliar situation a defensive process is activated, akin to the detachment that develops in young children undergoing major separations (Ainsworth & Bell, 1970; Ainsworth et al., 1978). Although the avoidant infants had themselves experienced no major separations, their mothers had tended to be rejecting at home during the first year, especially when their babies sought contact, as well as being generally insensitive to infant signals.

In regard to socialization, the findings suggest that infants have a natural behavioral disposition to comply with the wishes of the principal attachment figure. This disposition emerges most clearly if the attachment figure is sensitively responsive to infant signals, whereas efforts to train and discipline the infant, instead of fostering the wished-for compliance, tend to work against it (Ainsworth, Bell, & Stayton, 1974; Stayton, Hogan, & Ainsworth, 1971).

All of these findings tend to be supportive of attachment theory, but one in particular supports our emphasis on the interaction of behavioral systems. Bretherton and Ainsworth (1974), in an analysis of the responses of 106 one-year-olds to a stranger in a strange situation, showed how such responses involve the interactions between the fear-wariness system and the affiliative (sociable) system activated by the stranger, and also affect attachment behavior directed toward the mother and exploration of the toys. For example, nearly all babies manifested both sociability to the stranger and some degree of fear or wariness—the more of one, the less of the other. Few displayed only fear with no sociability, and very few displayed only sociability and no fear. Publication of these and other findings was interspersed with theoretical expositions (e.g., Ainsworth, 1969, 1972, 1977, 1979).

Finally, the strange situation procedure highlighted the distinction between secure and insecure infants, and between two groups of insecure infants—avoidant and ambivalent-resistant. Much evidence emerged in our studies relating these differences to maternal caregiving behavior, but these are most comprehensively dealt with by Ainsworth, Bell, and Stayton (1971) and Ainsworth et al. (1978).

In the meantime John Bowlby, whose research group had received generous support from the Ford Foundation, and who from 1963 was himself supported by the United Kingdom Medical Research Council, was working on his *Attachment and Loss* volumes. This trilogy brought to fruition the themes introduced in his earlier papers. It was planned with the whole in mind, and is best viewed as a whole. The first volume, *Attachment*, was published in 1969. From the early 1960s he and Ainsworth were exchanging drafts of all major publications, making comments and suggestions, and were continually taking each other's work into account. Ainsworth's work, including the Ganda study and the early findings of the strange situation, were drawn on in Bowlby's first volume, which included her major contribution of the concept of a secure base and variations in the security of attachment shown by different children. At the same time, this volume had profound influence on her work. In it, Bowlby elaborated the ethological and evolutionary underpinnings of attachment theory, discarded drive theory, and in its place, developed the concept of behavioral systems as control systems designed to achieve a specified end, activated in certain conditions and terminated in others. Postulating a plurality of behavioral systems, Bowlby described interactions among them, for example the dovetailing of the infant's attachment system and the caregiving system of the adult, and the way the activation of attachment behavior often alternates with that of exploratory behavior. The control systems approach to attachment behavior emphasizes inner organization and the development of working models of attachment figures and the self, which permit the development of the goal-corrected partnership between child and mother during the preschool years.

The second volume of the trilogy dealt with separation (Bowlby, 1973). The first half expanded Bowlby's earlier papers about separation anxiety, and presented a theory of fear that was merely suggested earlier. Of particular interest is the proposal that a child is genetically disposed to respond with fear to certain stimuli, such as sudden movement and sharp changes in the level of light and sound that, although not being dangerous in themselves, are statistically associated with dangerous situations. These natural clues to potential danger, of which one is being alone, activate either escape behavior or attachment behavior, and usually both, and thus promote the individual's survival. In the second half of the volume, Bowlby dealt with anxious attachment, conditions that promote it, and the intimate relationship of anger to attachment-related anxiety. As clinical examples of anxious attachment he considered both "school phobias" of children and the agoraphobia of adults, and stressed cross-generational effects in the etiology of each.

Two very important chapters have too often been overlooked. One dealt with the essential link between secure attachment and the development of healthy self-reliance—of particular interest to Ainsworth because of its roots in the *secure base* concept. The other, entitled "Pathways for the Growth of Personality," based on Waddington's theory of epigenesis, emphasized the constant interaction between genetic and environmental influences in personality development.

The third volume of the trilogy was concerned with loss (Bowlby, 1980). Near the beginning of it he included one of the most basic chapters of the trilogy—entitled "An Information Processing Approach to Defence"—that is as pertinent to the earlier two volumes as it is to the third. Drawing on cognitive psychological concepts and research, he pointed out that much sensory input normally is evaluated quickly and unconsciously in terms of stored knowledge, and then excluded from the highest, conscious level of cognitive processing as a matter of sheer efficiency. Under other circumstances, when accessing stored experience to evaluate current input would occasion significant anxiety, there may be *defensive* exclusion of input before it can proceed to conscious processing. Attachment behavior and associated feelings are especially vulnerable to such exclusion. When the attachment system is intensely activated and is often or for an extended period not terminated, defensive exclusion is likely to occur. This results in the defence manifested by avoidant children and in the detachment attributable to severe separation experiences. Such exclusion may well occur in adults as a response to loss, and accounts for some of the pathological variants of mourning. In addition to defensive processes, this chapter includes a valuable discussion of internal working models of attachment figures and of the self, pointing out that there may be more than one model of each figure and that these may conflict.

In the second section of the volume, which dealt with the mourning of adults, Bowlby drew heavily on the works of Colin Murray Parkes (e.g., Parkes, 1972), who joined the research team in 1962. It described four phases of mourning: (a) numbing; (b) yearning for the lost figure, and anger; (c) disorganization and despair; and (d) finally, if all goes well, reorganization. Bowlby considered disorders of mourning together with conditions contributing to them. Finally, he examined the connection between loss and depression, with particular attention to the work of Brown and Harris (1978). The last section, which dealt with children's mourning, emphasized both the similarity of the processes involved in children's and adults' responses to loss, and the reasons why children may have particular difficulty in resolving their mourning by successful reorganization of their lives.

1980 TO 1990

Bowlby intended his contribution as an up-to-date version of psychoanalytic object-relations theory, compatible with contemporary ethology and evolution theory, supported by research, and helpful to clinicians in understanding and treating child and adult patients. Nevertheless, it was developmental psychologists rather than clinicians who first adopted attachment theory, having found both traditional psychoanalytic and social learning theory to provide inadequate theoretical and methodological guidelines for research into personality development. Psychotherapists at that time were relatively content with one or another existing version of psychoanalytic theory as a guide, perhaps relying more on technique than theory for their therapeutic successes.

In several articles Bowlby suggested explicit guidelines for treatment that had been implicit in attachment theory (e.g., Bowlby, 1988b). The therapist begins with an understanding of the patient's current difficulties, especially difficulties in interpersonal relations. He or she then tries to serve as a secure base, helping the patient build up trust enough to be able to explore current relationships, including relations with the therapist. The therapist recognizes that a patient's difficulties are likely to have their origin in real-life experiences, rather than in fantasies. The therapist thus seeks to guide the patient's explorations toward earlier experiences—especially, painful ones with parents—and to expectations about current relationships derived from the internal working models of self and attachment figure that have resulted, and so to consider how these models, perhaps appropriate to the earlier situation, may be giving rise to feelings and actions inappropriate in the present. This review of past experiences is likely to lead to a reevaluation of them, a revision of working models, and gradually, to improved interpersonal relations in the here and now.

A second aspect of Bowlby's effort to draw attachment theory to the attention of clinicians was his acceptance of many invitations to speak at professional meetings throughout the world. A number of the addresses were subsequently published in professional journals or drawn together in collections (e.g., Bowlby, 1979, 1988a). Now, consequently, the clinical group that he originally wanted to reach undoubtedly outnumbers his devoted group of developmental researchers.

Finally, Bowlby's most recent contribution was a new biography of Charles Darwin (Bowlby, 1990). Long an admirer of Darwin, who esteemed his theory of evolution as a keystone in an ethological approach to personality development, Bowlby turned to applying attachment theory to an understanding of the chronic ill health that plagued Darwin. Darwin's mother had become seriously ill when he was very young, and died when he was eight years old. Bowlby cited evidence to show that Darwin never had been able fully to mourn her death. Bowlby maintained that this left him as an adult sensitized to real or threatened losses of family members, and accounted for his psychological symptoms in terms of attachment theory (Bowlby, 1990).

Ainsworth in 1975–1976, nearing the completion of the publication of the findings of her Baltimore study, accepted an appointment at the University of Virginia and began work with a new generation of students, and continued her interest (sometimes participation) in the work of former students and colleagues. This subsequent research has substantially extended the field, inspired by the larger vistas opened by the latter two volumes of Bowlby's trilogy. Attachment research, which usually used infant attachment classification as a base line, has been moving increasingly into the preschool years, adolescence, and adulthood. Two sets of researchers should be mentioned especially. Alan Sroufe of the University of Minnesota and his students and colleagues have been undertaking long-term longitudinal follow-ups to ascertain the effect of the security or insecurity of infant–mother attachment on children's performance of later developmental tasks, and to identify conditions that alter expected performance. Mary Main of the University of California at Berkeley and her students and colleagues have focused on devising new procedures for assessing attachment at later ages—specifically at age six and in adulthood. Her Adult Attachment Interview has proved to be useful with adolescents as well as adults, and promises to be very useful in clinical research. Another extension of attachment research of special interest to clinicians is the application of current techniques to understand the ways in which attachment develops in various at-risk populations.

Thus, current attachment research has made progress in elucidating conditions that affect the extent to which an individual remains on an initial developmental pathway or shifts direction at one or more points in development. It also is yielding support to Bowlby's emphasis on cross-generational effects. Ainsworth's own chief original contribution in recent years has been to extend ethologically oriented attachment theory to cover attachments and affectional bonds other than those between parents and their offspring, in the hope that this can be a theoretical guideline for future research into other interpersonal aspects important in personality development (e.g., Ainsworth, 1989; in press).

In conclusion, we feel fortunate indeed in the outcome of our partnership in an ethological approach to personality development. At first rejected by theoreticians, clinicians, and researchers alike, the intertwining of an open-ended theory and research both guided by it and enriching it has come to be viewed by many as fruitful. Focusing on intimate interpersonal relations, attachment theory does not aspire to address all aspects of personality development. However, it is an open-ended theory and, we hope, open enough to be able to comprehend new findings that result from other approaches. From its outset it has been eclectic, drawing on a number of scientific disciplines, including developmental, cognitive, social, and personality psychology, systems theory, and various branches of biological science, including genetics. Although, at present, attachment theory leaves open many questions, both theoretical and practical, we are confident that attachment theorists will continue to be alert to new developments, in these and other areas, that will help to provide answers to problems still outstanding.

References

Ainsworth, M. D. (1962). The effects of maternal deprivation: A review of findings and controversy in the context of research strategy. In *Deprivation of maternal care: A reassessment of its effects* (Public Health Papers, No. 15, pp. 87–195). Geneva, Switzerland: World Health Organization.

Ainsworth, M. D. (1963). The development of mother–infant interaction among the Ganda. In B. M. Foss (Ed.), *Determinants of infant behaviour* (Vol. 2, pp. 67–112). London: Methuen.

Ainsworth, M. D. S. (1967). *Infancy in Uganda: Infant care and the growth of love.* Baltimore: Johns Hopkins University Press.

Ainsworth, M. D. S. (1969). Object relations, dependency and attachment: A theoretical review of the infant–mother relationship. *Child Development, 40,* 969–1025.

Ainsworth, M. D. S. (1972). Attachment and dependency: A comparison. In J. L. Gewirtz (Ed.), *Attachment and dependency* (pp. 97–137). Washington, DC: Winston.

Ainsworth, M. D. S. (1977). Attachment theory and its utility in cross-cultural research. In P. H. Leiderman, S. R. Tulkin, & A. Rosenfeld (Eds.), *Culture and infancy: Variations in the human experience* (pp. 49–67). San Diego, CA: Academic Press.

Ainsworth, M. D. S. (1979). Attachment as related to mother–child interaction. In J. S. Rosenblatt, R. A. Hinde, C. Beer, & M. Busnel (Eds.), *Advances in the study of behavior* (Vol. 9, pp. 1–51). San Diego, CA: Academic Press.

Ainsworth, M. D. S. (1989). Attachments beyond infancy. *American Psychologist, 44,* 709–716.

Ainsworth, M. D. S. (in press). Attachments and other affectional bonds across the life cycle. In C. M. Parkes, J. Stevenson-Hinde, & P. Marris (Eds.), *Attachment across the life cycle.* New York: Routledge.

Ainsworth, M. D., & Ainsworth, L. H. (1958). *Measuring security in personal adjustment.* Toronto, Canada: University of Toronto Press.

Ainsworth, M. D. S., & Bell, S. M. (1969). Some contemporary patterns of mother–infant interaction in the feeding situation. In A. Ambrose (Ed.), *Stimulation in early infancy* (pp. 133–170). San Diego, CA: Academic Press.

Ainsworth, M. D. S., & Bell, S. M. (1970). Attachment, exploration, and separation: Individual differences in strange-situation behavior of one-year-olds. *Child Development, 41,* 49–67.

Ainsworth, M. D. S., Bell, S. M., & Stayton, D. J. (1971). Individual differences in the strange-situation behavior of one-year-olds. In H. R. Schaffer (Ed.), *The origins of human social relations* (pp. 17–58). San Diego, CA: Academic Press.

Ainsworth, M. D. S., Bell, S. M., & Stayton, D. J. (1974). Infant–mother attachment and social development: Socialisation as a product of reciprocal responsiveness to signals. In M. J. M. Richards (Ed.), *The integration of a child into a social world* (pp. 99–135). London: Cambridge University Press.

Ainsworth, M. D. S., Blehar, M. C., Waters, E., & Wall, S. (1978). *Patterns of attachment: A psychological study of the strange situation.* Hillsdale, NJ: Erlbaum.

Ainsworth, M. D., & Bowlby, J. (1953). *Research strategy in the study of mother–child separation.* Paris: Courrier de la Centre International de l'Enfance.

Ainsworth, M. D. S., & Wittig, B. A. (1969). Attachment and exploratory behaviour of one-year-olds in a strange situation. In B. M. Foss (Ed.), *Determinants of infant behaviour* (Vol. 4, pp. 111–136). London: Methuen.

Bell, S. M., & Ainsworth, M. D. S. (1972). Infant crying and maternal responsiveness. *Child Development, 43,* 1171–1190.

Blatz, W. E. (1966). *Human security: Some reflections.* Toronto, Canada: University of Toronto Press.

Bowlby, J. (1944). Forty-four juvenile thieves: Their characters and their home life. *International Journal of Psycho-Analysis, 25,* 19–52, 107–127.

Bowlby, J. (1951). *Maternal care and mental health.* Geneva, Switzerland: World Health Organization.

Bowlby, J. (1953). Some pathological processes set in train by early mother–child separation. *Journal of Mental Science, 2,* 265–272.

Bowlby, J. (1958). The nature of a child's tie to his mother. *International Journal of Psycho-Analysis, 39,* 350–373.

Bowlby, J. (1960a). Grief and mourning in infancy and early childhood. *Psychoanalytic Study of the Child, 15,* 9–52.

Bowlby, J. (1960b). Separation anxiety. *International Journal of Psycho-Analysis, 41,* 89–113.

Bowlby, J. (1961a). Processes of mourning. *International Journal of Psycho-Analysis, 42,* 317–340.

Bowlby, J. (1961b). Separation anxiety: A critical review of the literature. *Journal of Child Psychology and Psychiatry, 1,* 251–269.

Bowlby, J. (1963). Pathological mourning and childhood mourning. *Journal of the American Psychoanalytic Association, 11,* 500–541.

Bowlby, J. (1969). *Attachment and loss: Vol. 1. Attachment.* New York: Basic Books.

Bowlby, J. (1973). *Attachment and loss: Vol. 2. Separation: Anxiety and anger.* New York: Basic Books.

Bowlby, J. (1979). *The making and breaking of affectional bonds.* London: Tavistock.

Bowlby, J. (1980). *Attachment and loss: Vol. 3. Loss: Sadness and depression.* New York: Basic Books.

Bowlby, J. (1988a). *A secure base.* New York: Basic Books.

Bowlby, J. (1988b). Attachment, communication, and the therapeutic process. In J. Bowlby, *A secure base* (pp. 137–157). New York: Basic Books.

Bowlby, J. (1990). *Charles Darwin: A new biography.* London: Hutchinson.

Bowlby, J., & Ainsworth, M. D. S. (1965). *Child care and the growth of love* (2nd ed.). Harmondsworth, England: Penguin Books.

Bowlby, J., Ainsworth, M. D., Boston, M., & Rosenbluth, D. (1956). Effects of mother–child separation. *British Journal of Medical Psychology, 29,* 169–201.

Bretherton, I., & Ainsworth, M. D. S. (1974). Responses of one-year-olds to a stranger in a strange situation. In M. Lewis & L. A. Rosenblum (Eds.), *The origin of fear* (pp. 131–164). New York: Wiley.

Brown, G. W., & Harris, T. (1978). *The social origins of depression: A study of psychiatric disorder in women.* London: Tavistock.

Heinicke, C. (1956). Some effects of separating two-year-old children from their parents. *Human Relations, 9,* 105–176.

Heinicke, C., & Westheimer, I. (1966). *Brief separations.* New York: International Universities Press.

Klopfer, B., Ainsworth, M. D., Klopfer, W. G., & Holt, R. R. (1954). *Developments in the Rorschach technique* (Vol. 1). Yonkers-on-Hudson, NY: World Book.

Parkes, C. M. (1972). *Studies of grief in adult life.* New York: International Universities Press.

Robertson, J. (1952). *A two-year-old goes to hospital* [Film]. New York: New York University Film Library.

Robertson, J., & Bowlby, J. (1952). Responses of young children to separation from their mothers. *Courrier de la Centre International de l'Enfance, 2,* 131–142.

Salter, M. D. (1940). *An evaluation of adjustment based on the concept of security* (University of Toronto Studies, Child Development Series, No. 18). Toronto, Canada: University of Toronto Press.

Stayton, D. J., & Ainsworth, M. D. S. (1973). Individual differences in infant responses to brief, everyday separations as related to other infant and maternal behavior. *Developmental Psychology, 9,* 226–235.

Stayton, D. J., Ainsworth, M. D. S., & Main, M. (1973). The development of separation behavior in the first year of life: Protest, following, and greeting. *Developmental Psychology, 9,* 213–225.

Stayton, D.J., Hogan, R., & Ainsworth, M. D. S. (1971). Infant obedience and maternal behavior: The origins of socialization reconsidered. *Child Development, 42,* 1057–1069.

PART 2
Discussion Questions

1. Summarize the major historical moments in the conceptual formulation of attachment theory as we know it today.

2. Both Bowlby and Ainsworth drew on a number of scientific disciplines in formulating their research. What are the main concepts they borrowed from these disciplines and how are they synthesized in the theory?

3. What sources of evidence did Bowlby and Ainsworth use to formulate their theory? Specifically, explain the various roles that direct observations, case studies, and experimentation played in gathering the evidence they needed. In your opinion, did the methods they used follow the standard procedures generally used in science?

4. In their article, Ainsworth and Bowlby stated that "the Strange Situation procedure soon became widely used, if not always wisely and well, and has quite overshadowed the findings of the research project that gave rise to it and on which its validity depended." What were the original findings they refer to and in what ways could an overemphasis on the evaluation of attachment security blur the central message of the theory?

5. The origins of attachment theory date back to the 1940's and were mainly derived from observations of mothers and their infants. However, today's infants are often exposed to more than one caregiver. Could attachment theory be used to describe: a) attachments between infants and fathers or male caregivers; and b) attachments between working mothers and infants who attend day care?

6. One of the central concepts of attachment theory is that of *secure base* and *secure base use*. Do you see any utility in using this concept for studying social relationships beyond infancy, and possibly in adulthood?

Suggested Readings

Ainsworth, M. D. S., Blehar, M. D., Waters, E., & Wall, S. (1978). *Patterns of Attachment: A Psychological Study of the Strange Situation.* Hillsdale, NJ: Erlbaum.

Bowlby, J. (1969). *Attachment and Loss: Attachment.* New York: Basic Books.

Bowlby, J. (1977). The making and breaking of affectional bonds. *British Journal of Psychiatry, 130,* 201–210.

Bretherton, I. (1992). The origins of attachment theory: John Bowlby and Mary Ainsworth. *Developmental Psychology, 28* (5), 759–775.

Sroufe, L. A. & Waters, E. (1977). Attachment as an organizational construct. *Child Development, 48,* 1184–1199.

MODULE 12

HARRY HARLOW'S EXPERIMENTS ON THE AFFECTIONAL RESPONSES OF THE YOUNG INFANT

Although John Bowlby's theory of attachment is widely accepted, it has been preceded by several other theories that proposed different processes to explain the same phenomenon. This article by Harry Harlow marked a turning point in the history of research on the topic of attachment. In fact, the empirical evidence it brought forth provided many of the essential ingredients Bowlby used to formulate his theory of attachment. In the first part of this module, you will learn how Harlow's experiments with young rhesus monkeys shed new light on the origin of the first affectional bond at a time when the dominant explanations for this phenomenon were those offered by the psychoanalytic and the social learning theories. In the second part you will discuss and assess the value of Harry Harlow's contribution to our current understanding of the processes giving rise to infant–mother attachment.

INTRODUCTION

In 1958, when Harry Harlow published his paper *The Nature of Love*, the dominant theories held that the infant-mother tie is either secondary to the oral needs of the infant, or to primary drive gratification. The two theories, psychoanalytic and social learning, respectively, both proposed that the infant has no primary disposition to become attached to the mother, and that attachment derives from the more primary need for food. In her exposition of this view, Anna Freud explained that the first affective experience of the newborn consists of the positive pleasure associated with hunger satiation. This is so because in this initial stage, prior to ego differentiation from the id, the newborn does not distinguish self from non-self and sexual energy is thus narcissistically invested in the experience of bodily pleasure. With some ego differentiation, the baby now becomes capable of investing her libido in the food itself. The infant now *loves* the milk, breast or bottle. In the final stage, with the capacity to form internal representations, this love is now transferred to the provider of food who becomes an object of desire in and of herself. Because this theory focuses on the objects in which the libido is successively invested as the infant goes through the three stages just described, this proposal on the origin of infant–mother attachment was called *object-relation theory*.

In the early 1950's, social learning theorists also proposed their own theory of attachment. The term they used to describe the phenomenon was *dependency*, and their theory aimed to explain how a drive for dependency was acquired. They began by observing that the newborn is helplessly dependent upon the mother for the gratification of her primary drives or basic physiological needs. When in a primary drive state (e.g., hunger), the crying infant is reinforced by the nurturing actions of mother. Thus, during the first year of life, cues received from the mother are repeatedly associated with the primary reward of feeding, with the result that the infant learns to attach a strong reinforcement value to the nearness of the mother. In this way, proximity seeking (a manifestation of dependency) eventually emerges as a secondary drive.

Dollar and Miller first proposed the theory that all motives (drives) for sociability, dependence, and need to receive and show affection are learned through a similar mechanism. They also suggested that with development, seeking proximity to the mother could become generalized to others and that, in the process, *tertiary drives* could be formed, including, approval seeking and attention seeking. Not surprisingly, during the 1950's, child psychologists advised mothers against responding too quickly to the cries and bids for attention of their infants as, by these responses, they could compromise the formation of a strong personality and instead encourage the emergence of dependency traits.

Commenting on the fact that his contemporary psychologists were denying that love could be a real motive for attachment behaviors, Harlow observed that this assumption stood "in sharp contrast with the attitude taken by many famous and normal people," regarding the young infant. Accordingly, he proposed that the strong affective bond that develops between the infant and the mother may not be an indirect product of more basic needs and that, in humans, and indeed, in all mammalian species, the need for love and affection may be as primary as is the need of food. It is this shocking proposal that Harlow set out to test experimentally in the series of experiments reported in his paper *The Nature of Love*. Before you read this article, reproduced in Part 1, we encourage you to read the discussion questions in Part 2.

PART 1
REQUIRED READING

THE NATURE OF LOVE[1]

Harry F. Harlow
University of Wisconsin

---

[1]Address of the President at the sixty-sixth Annual Convention of the American Psychological Association, Washington, D.C., August 31, 1958.

The researches reported in this paper were supported by funds supplied by Grant No. M-722, National Institutes of Health, by a grant from the Ford Foundation, and by funds received from the Graduate School of the University of Wisconsin.

Love is a wondrous state, deep, tender, and rewarding. Because of its intimate and personal nature it is regarded by some as an improper topic for experimental research. But, whatever our personal feelings may be, our assigned mission as psychologists is to analyze all facets of human and animal behavior into their component variables. So far as love or affection is concerned, psychologists have failed in this mission. The little we know about love does not transcend simple observation, and the little we write about it has been written better by poets and novelists. But of greater concern is the fact that psychologists tend to give progressively less attention to a motive which pervades our entire lives. Psychologists, at least psychologists who write textbooks, not only show no interest in the origin and development of love or affection, but they seem to be unaware of its very existence.

The apparent repression of love by modern psychologists stands in sharp contrast with the attitude taken by many famous and normal people. The word "love" has the highest reference frequency of any word cited in Bartlett's book of *Familiar Quotations*. It would appear that this emotion has long had a vast interest and fascination for human beings, regardless of the attitude taken by psychologists; but the quotations cited, even by famous and normal people, have a mundane redundancy. These authors and authorities have stolen love from the child and infant and made it the exclusive property of the adolescent and adult.

Thoughtful men, and probably all women, have speculated on the nature of love. From the developmental point of view, the general plan is quite clear: The initial love responses of the human being are those made by the infant to the mother or some mother surrogate. From this intimate attachment of the child to the mother, multiple learned and generalized affectional responses are formed.

Unfortunately, beyond these simple facts we know little about the fundamental variables underlying the formation of affectional responses and little about the mechanisms through which the love of the infant for the mother develops into the multifaceted response patterns characterizing love or affection in the adult. Because of the dearth of experimentation, theories about the fundamental nature of affection have evolved at the level of observation, intuition, and discerning guesswork, whether these have been proposed by psychologists, sociologists, anthropologists, physicians, or psychoanalysts.

The position commonly held by psychologists and sociologists is quite clear: The basic motives are, for the most part, the primary drives—particularly hunger, thirst, elimination, pain, and sex—and all other motives, including love or affection, are derived or secondary drives. The mother is associated with the reduction of the primary drives—particularly hunger, thirst, and pain—and through learning, affection or love is derived.

It is entirely reasonable to believe that the mother through association with food may become a secondary-reinforcing agent, but this is an inadequate mechanism to account for the persistence of the infant-maternal ties. There is a spate of researches on the formation of secondary reinforcers to hunger and thirst reduction. There can be no question that almost any external stimulus can become a secondary reinforcer if properly associated with tissue-need reduction, but the fact remains that this redundant literature demonstrates unequivocally that such derived drives suffer relatively rapid experimental extinction. Contrariwise, human affection does not extinguish when the mother ceases to have intimate association with the drives in question. Instead, the affectional ties to the mother show a lifelong, unrelenting persistence and, even more surprising, widely expanding generality.

Oddly enough, one of the few psychologists who took a position counter to modern psychological dogma was John B. Watson, who believed that love was an innate emotion elicited by cutaneous stimulation of the erogenous zones. But experimental psychologists, with their peculiar propensity to discover facts that are not true, brushed this theory aside by demonstrating that the human neonate had no differentiable emotions, and they established a fundamental psychological law that prophets are without honor in their own profession.

The psychoanalysts have concerned themselves with the problem of the nature of the development of love in the neonate and infant, using ill and aging human beings as subjects. They have discovered the overwhelming importance of the breast and related this to the oral erotic tendencies developed at an age preceding their subjects' memories. Their theories range from a belief that the infant has an innate need to achieve and suckle at the breast to beliefs not unlike commonly accepted psychological theories. There are exceptions, as seen in the recent writings of John Bowlby, who attributes importance not only to food and thirst satisfaction, but also to "primary object-clinging," a need for intimate physical contact, which is initially associated with the mother.

As far as I know, there exists no direct experimental analysis of the relative importance of the stimulus variables determining the affectional or love responses in the neonatal and infant primate. Unfortunately, the human neonate is a limited experimental subject for such researches because of his inadequate motor capabilities. By the time the human infant's motor responses can be precisely measured, the antecedent determining conditions cannot be defined, having been lost in a jumble and jungle of confounded variables.

Many of these difficulties can be resolved by the use of the neonatal and infant macaque monkey as the subject for the analysis of basic affectional variables. It is possible to make precise measurements in this primate beginning at two to ten days of age, depending upon the maturational status of the individual animal at birth. The macaque infant differs from the human infant in that the monkey is more mature at birth and grows more rapidly; but the basic responses relating to affection, including nursing, contact, clinging, and even visual and auditory exploration, exhibit no fundamental differences in the two species. Even the development of perception, fear, frustration, and learning capability follows very similar sequences in rhesus monkeys and human children.

Three years' experimentation before we started our studies on affection gave us experience with the neonatal monkey. We had separated more than 60 of these animals from their mothers 6 to 12 hours after birth and suckled them on tiny bottles. The infant mortality was only a small fraction of what would have obtained had we let the monkey mothers raise their infants. Our bottle-fed babies were healthier and heavier than monkey-mother-reared infants. We know that we are better monkey mothers than are real monkey mothers thanks to synthetic diets, vitamins, iron extracts, penicillin, chloromycetin, 5% glucose, and constant, tender, loving care.

During the course of these studies we noticed that the laboratory-raised babies showed strong attachment to the cloth pads (folded gauze diapers) which were used to cover the hardware-cloth floors of their cages. The infants clung to these pads and engaged in violent temper tantrums when the pads were removed and replaced for sanitary reasons. Such contact-need or responsiveness had been reported previously by Gertrude van Wagenen for the monkey and by Thomas McCulloch and George Haslerud for the chimpanzee and is reminiscent of the devotion often exhibited by human infants to their pillows, blankets, and soft, cuddly stuffed toys. Responsiveness by the one-day-old infant monkey to the cloth pad is shown in Figure 1, and an unusual and strong attachment of a six-month-old infant to the cloth pad is illustrated in Figure 2. The baby, human or monkey, if it is to survive, must clutch at more than a straw.

We had also discovered during some allied observational studies that a baby monkey raised on a bare wire-mesh cage floor survives with difficulty, if at all, during the first five days of life. If a wire-mesh cone is introduced, the baby does better; and, if the cone is covered with terry cloth, husky, healthy, happy babies evolve. It takes more than a baby and a box to make a normal monkey. We were impressed by the possibility that, above and beyond the bubbling fountain of breast or bottle, contact comfort might be a very important variable in the development of the infant's affection for the mother.

At this point we decided to study the development of affectional responses of neonatal and infant monkeys to an artificial, inanimate mother, and so we built a surrogate mother which we hoped and believed would be a good surrogate mother. In devising this surrogate mother we were dependent neither upon the capriciousness of evolutionary processes nor upon mutations produced by chance radioactive fallout. Instead, we designed the mother surrogate in terms of modern human-engineering principles. We produced a perfectly proportioned, streamlined body stripped of unnecessary bulges and appendices. Redun-dancy in the surrogate mother's system was avoided by reducing the number of breasts from two to one and placing this unibreast in an upper-thoracic, sagittal position, thus maximizing the natural and

FIGURE 5

Time spent on cloth and wire mother surrogates.

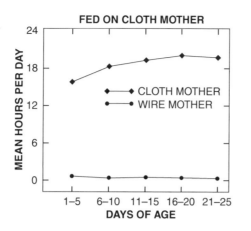
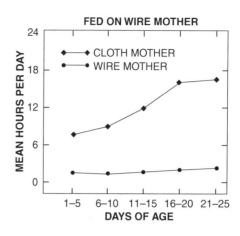

known perceptual-motor capabilities of the infant operator. The surrogate was made from a block of wood, covered with sponge rubber, and sheathed in tan cotton terry cloth. A light bulb behind her radiated heat. The result was a mother, soft, warm, and tender, a mother with infinite patience, a mother available twenty-four hours a day, a mother that never scolded her infant and never struck or bit her baby in anger. Furthermore, we designed a mother-machine with maximal maintenance efficiency since failure of any system or function could be resolved by the simple substitution of black boxes and new component parts. It is our opinion that we engineered a very superior monkey mother, although this position is not held universally by the monkey fathers.

Before beginning our initial experiment we also designed and constructed a second mother surrogate, a surrogate in which we deliberately built less than the maximal capability for contact comfort. This surrogate mother is illustrated in Figure 4. She is made of wire-mesh, a substance entirely adequate to provide postural support and nursing capability, and she is warmed by radiant heat. Her body differs in no essential way from that of the cloth mother surrogate other than in the quality of the contact comfort which she can supply.

In our initial experiment, the dual mother-surrogate condition, a cloth mother and a wire mother were placed in different cubicles attached to the infant's living cage as shown in Figure 4. For four newborn monkeys the cloth mother lactated and the wire mother did not; and, for the other four, this condition was reversed. In either condition the infant received all its milk through the mother surrogate as soon as it was able to maintain itself in this way, a capability achieved within two or three days except in the case of very immature infants. Supplementary feedings were given until the milk intake from the mother surrogate was adequate. Thus, the experiment was designed as a test of the relative importance of the variables of contact comfort and nursing comfort. During the first 14 days of life the monkey's cage floor was covered with a heating pad wrapped in a folded gauze diaper, and thereafter the cage floor was bare. The infants were always free to leave the heating pad or cage floor to contact either mother, and the time spent on the surrogate mothers was automatically recorded. Figure 5 shows the total time spent on the cloth and wire mothers under the two conditions of feeding. These data make it obvious that contact comfort is a variable of overwhelming importance in the development of affectional responses, whereas lactation is a variable of negligible importance. With age and opportunity to learn, subjects with the lactating wire mother showed decreasing responsiveness to her and increasing responsiveness to the nonlactating cloth mother, a finding completely contrary to any interpretation of derived drive in which the mother-form becomes conditioned to hunger-thirst reduction. The persistence of these differential responses throughout 165 consecutive days of testing is evident in Figure 6.

One control group of neonatal monkeys was raised on a single wire mother, and a second control group was raised on a single cloth mother. There were no differences between these two groups in amount of milk ingested or in weight

FIGURE 6

Long-term contact time on cloth and wire mother surrogates.

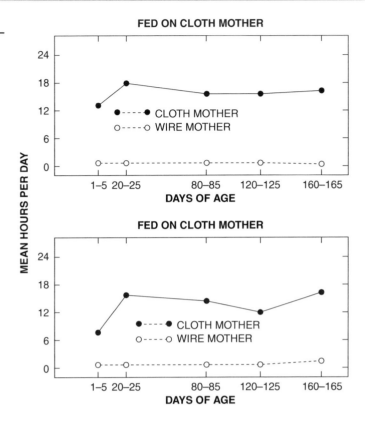

gain. The only difference between the groups lay in the composition of the feces, the softer stools of the wire-mother infants suggesting psychosomatic involvement. The wire mother is biologically adequate but psychologically inept.

We were not surprised to discover that contact comfort was an important basic affectional or love variable, but we did not expect it to overshadow so completely the variable of nursing; indeed, the disparity is so great as to suggest that the primary function of nursing as an affectional variable is that of insuring frequent and intimate body contact of the infant with the mother. Certainly, man cannot live by milk alone. Love is an emotion that does not need to be bottle- or spoon-fed, and we may be sure that there is nothing to be gained by giving lip service to love.

A charming lady once heard me describe these experiments; and, when I subsequently talked to her, her face brightened with sudden insight: "Now I know what's wrong with me," she said, "I'm just a wire mother." Perhaps she was lucky. She might have been a wire wife.

We believe that contact comfort has long served the animal kingdom as a motivating agent for affectional responses. Since at the present time we have no experimental data to substantiate this position, we supply information which must be accepted, if at all, on the basis of face validity:

One function of the real mother, human or subhuman, and presumably of a mother surrogate, is to provide a haven of safety for the infant in times of fear and danger. The frightened or ailing child clings to its mother, not its father; and this selective responsiveness in times of distress, disturbance, or danger may be used as a measure of the strength of affectional bonds. We have tested this kind of differential responsiveness by presenting to the infants in their cages, in the presence of the two mothers, various fear-producing stimuli such as the moving toy bear illustrated in Figure 13. A typical response to a fear stimulus is shown in Figure 14, and the data on differential responsiveness are presented in Figure 15. It is apparent that the cloth mother is highly preferred over the wire one, and this differential selectivity is enhanced by age and experience. In this situation, the variable of nursing appears to be of absolutely no importance; the infant consistently seeks the soft mother surrogate regardless of nursing condition.

Similarly, the mother or mother surrogate provides its young with a source of security, and this

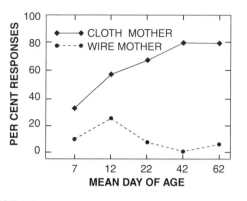

FIGURE 15

Differential responsiveness in fear tests.

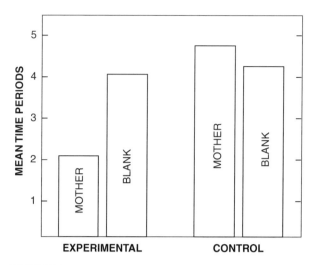

FIGURE 20

Emotionality index with and without the presence of the cloth mother.

role or function is seen with special clarity when mother and child are in a strange situation. At the present time we have completed tests for this relationship on four of our eight baby monkeys assigned to the dual mother-surrogate condition by introducing them for three minutes into the strange environment of a room measuring six feet by six feet by six feet (also called the "open-field test") and containing multiple stimuli known to elicit curiosity-manipulatory responses in baby monkeys. The subjects are placed in this situation twice a week for eight weeks with no mother surrogate present during alternate sessions and the cloth mother present during the others. A cloth diaper was always available as one of the stimuli throughout all sessions. After one or two adaptation sessions, the infants always rushed to the mother surrogate when she was present and clutched her, rubbed their bodies against her, and frequently manipulated her body and face. After a few additional sessions, the infants began to use the mother surrogate as a source of security, a base of operations. As is shown in Figures 16 and 17, they would explore and manipulate a stimulus and then return to the mother before adventuring again into the strange new world. The behavior of these infants was quite different when the mother was absent from the room. Frequently they would freeze in a crouched position, as is illustrated in Figures 18 and 19. Emotionality indices such as vocalization, crouching, rocking, and sucking increased sharply, as shown in Figure 20. Total emotionality score was cut in half when the mother was present. In the absence of the mother some of the experimental monkeys would rush to the center of the room where the mother was customarily placed and then run rapidly from object to object, screaming and crying all the while. Continuous, frantic clutching of their bodies was very common, even when not in the crouching position. These monkeys frequently contacted and clutched the cloth diaper, but this action never pacified them. The same behavior occurred in the presence of the wire mother. No difference between the cloth-mother-fed and wire-mother-fed infants was demonstrated under either condition. Four control infants never raised with a mother surrogate showed the same emotionality scores when the mother was absent as the experimental infants showed in the absence of the mother, but the controls' scores were slightly larger in the presence of the mother surrogate than in her absence.

Some years ago Robert Butler demonstrated that mature monkeys enclosed in a dimly lighted box would open and reopen a door hour after hour for no other reward than that of looking outside the box. We now have data indicating that neonatal monkeys show this same compulsive visual curiosity on their first test day in an adaptation of the Butler apparatus which we call the "love machine," an apparatus designed to measure love. Usually these tests are begun when the monkey is 10 days of age, but this same persistent visual exploration has been obtained in a three-day-old monkey during the first half-hour of testing. Butler also demonstrated that rhesus monkeys show

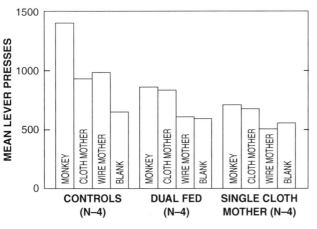

FIGURE 22

Differential responses to visual exploration.

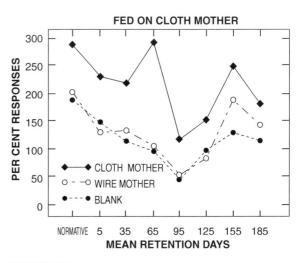

FIGURE 23

Retention of differential visual-exploration responses.

selectivity in rate and frequency of door-opening to stimuli of differential attractiveness in the visual field outside the box. We have utilized this principle of response selectivity by the monkey to measure strength of affectional responsiveness in our infants in the baby version of the Butler box. The test sequence involves four repetitions of a test battery in which four stimuli—cloth mother, wire mother, infant monkey, and empty box—are presented for a 30-minute period on successive days. The first four subjects in the dual mother-surrogate group were given a single test sequence at 40 to 50 days of age, depending upon the availability of the apparatus, and only their data are presented. The second set of four subjects is being given repetitive tests to obtain information relating to the development of visual exploration. The apparatus is illustrated in Figure 21. The data obtained from the first four infants raised with the two mother surrogates are presented in the middle graph of Figure 22 and show approximately equal responding to the cloth mother and another infant monkey, and no greater responsiveness to the wire mother than to an empty box. Again, the results are independent of the kind of mother that lactated, cloth or wire. The same results are found for a control group raised, but not fed, on a single cloth mother; these data appear in the graph on the right. Contrariwise, the graph on the left shows no differential responsiveness to cloth and wire mothers by a second control group, which was not raised on any mother surrogate. We can be certain that not all love is blind.

The first four infant monkeys in the dual mother-surrogate group were separated from their mothers between 165 and 170 days of age and tested for retention during the following 9 days and then at 30-day intervals for six successive months. Affectional retention as measured by the modified Butler box is given in Figure 23. In keeping with the data obtained on adult monkeys by Butler, we find a high rate of responding to any stimulus, even the empty box. But throughout the entire 185-day retention period there is a consistent and significant difference in response frequency to the cloth mother contrasted with either the wire mother or the empty box, and no consistent difference between wire mother and empty box.

Affectional retention was also tested in the open field during the first 9 days after separation and then at 30-day intervals, and each test condition was run twice at each retention interval. The infant's behavior differed from that observed during the period preceding separation. When the cloth mother was present in the post-separation period, the babies rushed to her, climbed up, clung tightly to her, and rubbed their heads and faces against her body. After this initial embrace and reunion, they played on the mother, including biting and tearing at her cloth cover; but they rarely made any attempt to leave her during the test period, nor did they manipulate or play with the objects in the room, in contrast with their behavior before maternal separation. The only exception was the occasional monkey that left the mother surrogate momentarily, grasped the folded piece

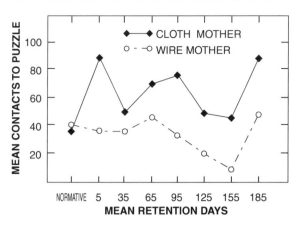

FIGURE 24

Retention of puzzle manipulation responsiveness.

of paper (one of the standard stimuli in the field), and brought it quickly back to the mother. It appeared that deprivation had enhanced the tie to the mother and rendered the contact-comfort need so prepotent that need for the mother overwhelmed the exploratory motives during the brief, three-minute test sessions. No change in these behaviors was observed throughout the 185-day period. When the mother was absent from the open field, the behavior of the infants was similar in the initial retention test to that during the preseparation tests; but they tended to show gradual adaptation to the open-field situation with repeated testing and, consequently, a reduction in their emotionality scores.

In the last five retention test periods, an additional test was introduced in which the surrogate mother was placed in the center of the room and covered with a clear Plexiglas box. The monkeys were initially disturbed and frustrated when their explorations and manipulations of the box failed to provide contact with the mother. However, all animals adapted to the situation rather rapidly. Soon they used the box as a place of orientation for exploratory and play behavior, made frequent contacts with the objects in the field, and very often brought these objects to the Plexiglas box. The emotionality index was slightly higher than in the condition of the available cloth mothers, but it in no way approached the emotionality level displayed when the cloth mother was absent. Obviously, the infant monkeys gained emotional security by the presence of the mother even though contact was denied.

Affectional retention has also been measured by tests in which the monkey must unfasten a three-device mechanical puzzle to obtain entrance into a compartment containing the mother surrogate. All the trials are initiated by allowing the infant to go through an unlocked door, and in half the trials it finds the mother present and in half, an empty compartment. The door is then locked and a ten-minute test conducted. In tests given prior to separation from the surrogate mothers, some of the infants had solved this puzzle and others had failed. The data of Figure 24 show that on the last test before separation there were no differences in total manipulation under mother-present and mother-absent conditions, but striking differences exist between the two conditions throughout the post-separation test periods. Again, there is no interaction with conditions of feeding.

The over-all picture obtained from surveying the retention data is unequivocal. There is little, if any, waning of responsiveness to the mother throughout this five-month period as indicated by any measure. It becomes perfectly obvious that this affectional bond is highly resistant to forgetting and that it can be retained for very long periods of time by relatively infrequent contact reinforcement. During the next year, retention tests will be conducted at 90-day intervals, and further plans are dependent upon the results obtained. It would appear that affectional responses may show as much resistance to extinction as has been previously demonstrated for learned fears and learned pain, and such data would be in keeping with those of common human observation.

The infant's responses to the mother surrogate in the fear tests, the open-field situation, and the baby Butler box and the responses on the retention tests cannot be described adequately with words. For supplementary information we turn to the motion picture record. (At this point a 20-minute film was presented illustrating and supplementing the behaviors described thus far in the address.)

We have already described the group of four control infants that had never lived in the presence of any mother surrogate and had demonstrated no sign of affection or security in the presence of the cloth mothers introduced in test sessions. When these infants reached the age of 250 days, cubicles containing both a cloth mother and a wire mother were attached to their cages. There was no lactation in these mothers, for the monkeys were on a solid-food diet. The initial reaction of the monkeys to the alterations was one of extreme disturbance. All the infants screamed violently and made repeated attempts to escape the cage whenever the door was opened. They kept a maximum distance from the mother surrogates and exhibited a considerable amount of rocking and crouching behavior, indicative of emotionality. Our first thought was that the critical period for the development of maternally directed affection had passed and that these macaque children were doomed to live as affectional orphans. Fortunately, these behaviors continued for only 12 to 48 hours and then gradually ebbed, changing from indifference to active contact on, and exploration of, the surrogates. The home-cage behavior of these control monkeys slowly became similar to that of the animals raised with the mother surrogates from birth. Their manipulation and play on the cloth mother became progressively more vigorous to the point of actual mutilation, particularly during the morning after the cloth mother had been given her daily change of terry covering. The control subjects were now actively running to the cloth mother when frightened and had to be coaxed from her to be taken from the cage for formal testing.

Objective evidence of these changing behaviors is given in Figure 25, which plots the amount of time these infants spent on the mother surrogates. Within 10 days mean contact time is approximately nine hours, and this measure remains relatively constant throughout the next 30 days. Consistent with the results on the subjects reared from birth with dual mothers, these late-adopted infants spent less than one and one-half hours per day in contact with the wire mothers, and this activity level was relatively constant throughout the test sessions. Although the maximum time that the control monkeys spent on the cloth mother was only about half that spent by the original dual mother-surrogate group, we cannot be sure that this discrepancy is a function of differential early experience. The control monkeys were about three months older when the mothers were attached to their cages than the experimental animals had been when their mothers were removed and the retention tests begun. Thus, we do not know what the amount of contact would be for a

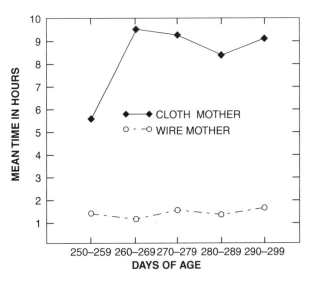

FIGURE 25

Differential time spent on cloth and wire mother surrogates by monkeys started at 250 days of age.

250-day-old animal raised from birth with surrogate mothers. Nevertheless, the magnitude of the differences and the fact that the contact-time curves for the mothered-from-birth infants had remained constant for almost 150 days suggest that early experience with the mother is a variable of measurable importance.

The control group has also been tested for differential visual exploration after the introduction of the cloth and wire mothers; these behaviors are plotted in Figure 26. By the second test session a high level of exploratory behavior had developed, and the responsiveness to the wire mother and the empty box is significantly greater than that to the cloth mother. This is probably not an artifact since there is every reason to believe that the face of the cloth mother is a fear stimulus to most monkeys that have not had extensive experience with this object during the first 40 to 60 days of life. Within the third test session a sharp change in trend occurs, and the cloth mother is then more frequently viewed than the wire mother or the blank box; this trend continues during the fourth session, producing a significant preference for the cloth mother.

Before the introduction of the mother surrogate into the home-cage situation, only one of the four control monkeys had ever contacted the cloth mother in the open-field tests. In general, the surro-

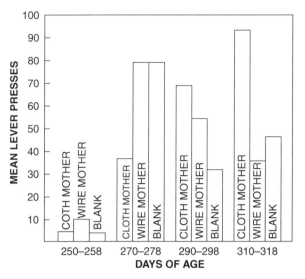

FIGURE 26

Differential visual exploration of monkeys started at 250 days of age.

gate mother not only gave the infants no security, but instead appeared to serve as a fear stimulus. The emotionality scores of these control subjects were slightly higher during the mother-present test sessions than during the mother-absent test sessions. These behaviors were changed radically by the fourth post-introduction test approximately 60 days later. In the absence of the cloth mothers the emotionality index in this fourth test remains near the earlier level, but the score is reduced by half when the mother is present, a result strikingly similar to that found for infants raised with the dual mother-surrogates from birth. The control infants now show increasing object exploration and play behavior, and they begin to use the mother as a base of operations, as did the infants raised from birth with the mother surrogates. However, there are still definite differences in the behavior of the two groups. The control infants do not rush directly to the mother and clutch her violently; but instead they go toward, and orient around, her, usually after an initial period during which they frequently show disturbed behavior, exploratory behavior, or both.

That the control monkeys develop affection or love for the cloth mother when she is introduced into the cage at 250 days of age cannot be questioned. There is every reason to believe, however, that this interval of delay depresses the intensity of the affectional response below that of the infant-monkeys that were surrogate-mothered from birth, onward. In interpreting these data it is well to remember that the control monkeys had had continuous opportunity to observe and hear other monkeys housed in adjacent cages and that they had had limited opportunity to view and contact surrogate mothers in the test situations, even though they did not exploit the opportunities.

During the last two years we have observed the behavior of two infants raised by their own mothers. Love for the real mother and love for the surrogate mother appear to be very similar. The baby macaque spends many hours a day clinging to its real mother. If away from the mother when frightened, it rushes to her and in her presence shows comfort and composure. As far as we can observe, the infant monkey's affection for the real mother is strong, but no stronger than that of the experimental monkey for the surrogate cloth mother, and the security that the infant gains from the presence of the real mother is no greater than the security it gains from a cloth surrogate. Next year we hope to put this problem to final, definitive, experimental test. But, whether the mother is real or a cloth surrogate, there does develop a deep and abiding bond between mother and child. In one case it may be the call of the wild and in the other the McCall of civilization, but in both cases there is "togetherness."

In spite of the importance of contact comfort, there is reason to believe that other variables of measurable importance will be discovered. Postural support may be such a variable, and it has been suggested that, when we build arms into the mother surrogate, 10 is the minimal number required to provide adequate child care. Rocking motion may be such a variable, and we are comparing rocking and stationary mother surrogates and inclined planes. The differential responsiveness to cloth mother and cloth-covered inclined plane suggests that clinging as well as contact to an affectional variable of importance. Sounds, particularly natural, maternal sounds, may operate as either unlearned or learned affectional variables. Visual responsiveness may be such a variable, and it is possible that some semblance of visual imprinting may develop in the neonatal monkey. There are indications that this becomes a variable of importance during the course of infancy through some maturational process.

John Bowlby has suggested that there is an affectional variable which he calls "primary object following," characterized by visual and oral search of the mother's face. Our surrogate-mother-raised baby monkeys are at first inattentive to her face, as are human neonates to human mother faces. But by 30 days of age ever-increasing responsiveness to the mother's face appears—whether through learning, maturation, or both—and we have reason to believe that the face becomes an object of special attention.

Our first surrogate-mother-raised baby had a mother whose head was just a ball of wood since the baby was a month early and we had not had time to design a more esthetic head and face. This baby had contact with the blank-faced mother for 180 days and was then placed with two cloth mothers, one motionless and one rocking, both being endowed with painted, ornamented faces. To our surprise the animal would compulsively rotate both faces 180 degrees so that it viewed only a round, smooth face and never the painted, ornamented face. Furthermore, it would do this as long as the patience of the experimenter in reorienting the faces persisted. The monkey showed no sign of fear or anxiety, but it showed unlimited persistence. Subsequently it improved its technique, compulsively removing the heads and rolling them into its cage as fast as they were returned. We are intrigued by this observation, and we plan to examine systematically the role of the mother face in the development of infant-monkey affections. Indeed, these observations suggest the need for a series of ethological-type researches on the two-faced female.

Although we have made no attempts thus far to study the generalization of infant-macaque affection or love, the techniques which we have developed offer promise in this uncharted field. Beyond this, there are few if any technical difficulties in studying the affection of the actual, living mother for the child, and the techniques developed can be utilized and expanded for the analysis and developmental study of father-infant and infant-infant affection.

Since we can measure neonatal and infant affectional responses to mother surrogates, and since we know they are strong and persisting, we are in a position to assess the effects of feeding and contractual schedules; consistency and inconsistency in the mother surrogates; and early, intermediate, and late maternal deprivation. Again, we have here a family of problems of fundamental interest and theoretical importance.

If the researches completed and proposed make a contribution, I shall be grateful; but I have also given full thought to possible practical applications. The socioeconomic demands of the present and the threatened socioeconomic demands of the future have led the American woman to displace, or threaten to displace, the American man in science and industry. If this process continues, the problem of proper child-rearing practices faces us with startling clarity. It is cheering in view of this trend to realize that the American male is physically endowed with all the really essential equipment to compete with the American female on equal terms in one essential activity: the rearing of infants. We now know that women in the working classes are not needed in the home because of their primary mammalian capabilities; and it is possible that in the foreseeable future neonatal nursing will not be regarded as a necessity, but as a luxury—to use Veblen's term—a form of conspicuous consumption limited perhaps to the upper classes. But whatever course history may take, it is comforting to know that we are now in contact with the nature of love.

PART 2
DISCUSSION QUESTIONS

1. How did Harlow justify using macaque monkeys to conduct research on the young infant's affectional system? Given these justifications, do you think anything valid concerning human babies can be learned through this kind of research?

2. How did Harlow test the validity of the behaviorist claim that love or affection are derived as secondary drives? First explain what is meant by this statement, then describe his research design, and summarize his findings.

3. One of the central concepts in modern attachment theory is that attachment, when successfully achieved, provides the infant with a secure basis for exploration. What empirical evidence did Harlow provide to support this proposal?

4. In your opinion, were the young monkeys that served as subjects in this research treated with adequate ethical standards? If you think they were not, how might researchers rectify these problems? What alternatives are available for researchers who seek to empirically examine the same questions?

5. Do these studies change the way you think about parenting? As compared to the views that prevailed concerning the origin of attachment behavior up to the 1950's, how do you think these studies subsequently affected parenting practices?

SUGGESTED READINGS

Ainsworth, M. D. S. (1969). Object relations, dependency, and attachment: A theoretical review of the infant–mother relationship. *Child Development, 40,* 969–1025.

Harlow, H. F., & Zimmerman, R. R. (1959). Affectional responses in the infant monkey. *Science, 130,* 421–432.

Harlow, H. F., & Harlow, M. K. (1965). The affectional systems. In A. M. Schrier, H. F. Harlow, & F. D. Tollnitz (Eds.), *Behavior of non human primates: Modern research trends.* Vol. 2. New York: Academic press, 1965, pp. 107–149.

Harlow, H. F., & Suomi, S. J. (1970). Nature of love: Simplified. *American Psychologist, 25,* 161–168.

MODULE 13

GENIE AND LANGUAGE ACQUISITION

In 1970, a modern day wild child was discovered. The case of Genie is now one of the most famous examples demonstrating the importance of both biological and environmental influences on language development. Genie was 13 years old when she was discovered in the basement of a California home, where she had been kept in virtual isolation, naked and harnessed to a potty seat for all of her early years. You will read about the case of Genie and explore the supporting evidence suggesting biological and environmental components in language acquisition.

■ INTRODUCTION

Is there a critical period for language acquisition? According to Noam Chomsky, children are born *hard wired* for language acquisition, and this biological endowment allows children to learn the various rule systems of language. This nativist perspective on language acquisition suggests that environmental influences are insufficient to explain for language acquisition and posits a critical period in which children are primed and ready to acquire language. Failing to develop language skills during this critical period makes it exceedingly difficult for a person to acquire language at a later point in development. In addition, certain regions of the brain have been identified as being especially important for language.

In contrast, the behaviorist/environmental perspective suggests that language is learned through conditioning and reinforcement. That is, children observe adults use language, model this behavior, get rewarded for uttering sequences of syllabus that sound like words in appropriate contexts and thus acquire language. Considerable research evidence questions this perspective, pointing to the failure of the behaviorist/environmentalist perspective to explain children's novel productions of language and the acquisition of the grammatical rules of language.

The interactionist perspective combines a biological and environmental perspective on language acquisition. This perspective suggests that there is a biological predisposition to learn language during the first years of childhood, but language acquisition requires environmental stimulation.

PART 1
Required Reading

The Civilizing of Genie

From Psychology Today, September 1981 by M. Pines. Copyright © 1981 by Maya Pines. Reprinted by permission of the author.

"In 1970, a wild child was found in California. Genie, now 24, has stirred up new questions about language and intelligence."

Maya Pines

Only a few cases are recorded of human beings who have grown up without any real contact with other humans. So rare is the phenomenon that when a 12-year-old "wild boy" was found in the forest of Aveyron in 18th-century France, the government ordered him brought to Paris to be examined by doctors in an institution for deaf-mutes. There he came under the care of the physician Jean Itard, who also acted as the boy's tutor. Itard left detailed records of his experience, which was later dramatized in the 1970 movie *The Wild Child*. Although the boy was not deaf, and despite Itard's work, the child never learned to speak.

In 1970, a wild child was found in California: a girl of 13 who had been isolated in a small room and had not been spoken to by her parents since infancy. "Genie," as she was later dubbed to protect her privacy by the psycholinguists who tested her, could not stand erect. At the time, she was unable to speak; she could only whimper.

The case came to light when Genie's 50-year-old mother ran away from her 70-year-old husband after a violent quarrel and took the child along. The mother was partially blind and applied for public assistance. The social worker in the welfare office took one look at Genie and called her supervisor, who called the police. Genie was sent to the Los Angeles Children's Hospital for tests. Charges of willful abuse were filed against both her parents, according to the *Los Angeles Times*. On the day he was due to appear in court, however, Genie's father shot himself to death. He left a note in which he wrote, "The world will never understand."

The discovery of Genie aroused intense curiosity among psychologists, linguists, neurologists, and others who study brain development. They were eager to know what Genie's mental level was at the time she was found and whether she would be capable of developing her faculties. "It's a terribly important case," says Harlan Lane, a psycholinguist at Northeastern University who wrote *The Wild Boy of Aveyron*. "Since our morality doesn't allow us to conduct deprivation experiments with human beings, these unfortunate people are all we have to go on."

Genie is now 24 years old. Through years of rehabilitation and special training, she has been observed and repeatedly tested. Hundreds of videotapes record her progress. She has been the subject of several journal articles and a book. Since the book was published in 1977, additional studies have brought into focus some of the issues raised by Genie's case. Far from settling any scientific controversies, she has provided fresh ammunition for arguments on both sides of a major issue: is there a "critical period" in a child's development during which, if language acquisition is not stimulated or encouraged, it may be impaired later on or not emerge at all? She has inspired a California researcher who worked with her, Susan Curtiss, to develop a controversial hypothesis about how language learning affects the two hemispheres of the brain. Genie has also stirred up debate about the relationship between language and other mental abilities. As a result, new research is now in progress on the surprising language ability of some mentally retarded children.

As described in Curtiss's book, *Genie: A Psycholinguistic Study of a Modern-Day "Wild Child"* (Academic Press), Genie is living proof of human resilience. It is surprising that she survived at all. Her father apparently hated children and tried to strangle Genie's mother while she was pregnant with her first child. According to Curtiss's book, when an earlier baby girl was born, he put the child in the garage because he couldn't stand her crying; the baby died of pneumonia at two-and-a-half months. A second child, a boy, died two days after birth, allegedly from choking on his own mucus. A third child was rescued and cared for by his grandmother when he was three years old and is still alive. Genie, the fourth child, was denied such help, however, because shortly after she was born, her grandmother was hit by a truck and killed.

From the age of 20 months, when her family moved into her grandmother's house, until she was 13 and a half, Genie lived in nearly total isolation. Curtiss's book and newspaper reports describe Genie's life at the time: naked and restrained by a harness that her father had fashioned, she was left to sit on her potty seat day after day. She could move only her hands and feet. She had nothing to do. At night, when she was not forgotten, she was put into a sort of straitjacket and caged in a crib that had wire-mesh sides and an overhead cover. She was often hungry.

If she made any noise, her father beat her. "He never spoke to her," wrote Curtiss." He made barking sounds and he growled at her.... Her mother was terrified of him—and besides, she was too blind to take much care of Genie. The task fell largely on Genie's brother, who, following his father's instructions, did not speak to Genie either. He fed her hurriedly and in silence, mostly milk and baby foods. There was little for Genie to listen to. Her mother and brother spoke in low voices for fear of her father.

When Genie arrived in Children's Hospital in November 1970, she was a pitiful, malformed, incontinent, unsocialized, and severely malnourished creature. Although she was beginning to show signs of pubescence, she weighed only 59 pounds. She could not straighten her arms or legs. She did not know how to chew. She salivated a great deal and spent much of her time spitting. And she was eerily silent.

Various physicians, psychologists, and therapists were brought in to examine her during those first months. Shortly after Genie was admitted as a patient, she was given the Vineland Social Maturity Scale and the Preschool Attainment Record, on which she scored as low as normal one-year-olds. At first, she seemed to recognize only her own name and the word sorry. After a while, she began to say two phrases that she used as if they were single words, in a ritualized way: stopit and nomore.

Psychologists at the hospital did not really know how much she understood. Nor did they know how to evaluate whatever language she had: to what degree did it deviate from the standard pattern? They eventually asked Victoria A. Fromkin, a UCLA psycholinguist, to study Genie's language abilities. Fromkin brought along a graduate student, Susan Curtiss (now an assistant professor of linguistics at UCLA), who became so fascinated by Genie that she devoted much of the next seven years of her life to researching the girl's linguistic development.

Working with Genie was not an easy task. Although she had learned to walk with a jerky motion and became more or less toilet trained during her first seven months at Children's Hospital, Genie still had many disconcerting habits. She salivated and spat constantly, so much so that her body and clothing were filled with spit and "reeked of a foul odor," as Curtiss recounts. When excited or agitated, she urinated, leaving her companion to deal with the results. And she masturbated excessively.

Nevertheless, Genie was decidedly human, and her delight at discovering the world—as well as her obvious progress—made the struggle worthwhile. When Curtiss started working with Genie, she began by simply spending time with her or taking her to visit places, in order to establish a relationship. She took Genie to the supermarket, where Genie walked around the store and examined the meats and the plastic containers with some curiosity. Every house seemed exciting to Genie, who had spent so much of her life cooped up in one room: on walks she would often go up to the front doors of houses, hoping that someone would open the door and let her in.

During her first seven months of freedom, Genie had learned to recognize many new words—probably hundreds by the time Curtiss started investigating her knowledge of language systematically in June 1971. And she had begun to speak. On a visit with Curtiss to the home of one of the therapists, Genie eagerly explored every room, then picked up a decorator pillow: when asked what it was, she replied "pillow." Asked if she wanted to see the family cat, Genie replied, "No. No. Cat," and shook her head vehemently. Most of the time, however, she said nothing.

At first Genie spoke only in one-word utterances, as toddlers do when they start to talk. Then in July of 1971, she began to string two words together on her own, not just while imitating what somebody else had said. She said "big teeth," "little marble," "two hand." A little later she produced some verbs "Curtiss come," "Want milk." In November of the same year she progressed to occasional three-word strings: "small two cup," "white clear box."

Unlike normal children, however, Genie never asked questions, despite many efforts to train her to do so. Nor did she understand much grammar. And her speech development was abnormally slow. A few weeks after normal children reach the two-word stage, their speech generally develops so rapidly and explosively that it is difficult to keep track of or describe. No such explosion occurred for Genie. Four years after she began to put words together, her speech remained, for the most part, like a somewhat garbled telegram.

While Genie did not speak in a fully developed, normal way, she acquired some language after she was discovered. That contradicted one aspect of the theory that says language can be learned only during a critical period between two years of age and puberty. According to Eric Lenneberg, a Harvard psychologist who put forth the theory in 1967, the brain of a child before the age of two is not sufficiently mature for the acquisition of language, while after puberty, when the brain's organization is complete, it has lost its flexibility and can no longer acquire a first language. Genie proved him wrong in one sense. Fromkin says, since the child "showed that a certain amount of language can be learned after the critical period."

On the other hand, Genie failed to learn the kind of grammatical principles that, according to Noam Chomsky, distinguish the language of human beings from that of animals. For example, she could not grasp the difference between various pronouns, or between active and passive verbs. In that sense, she appeared to suffer from having passed the critical period.

Her language deficiencies could not be attributed to a lack of teachers. Though at first it did not seem possible that she could ever attend any school, within a few months of her arrival at Children's Hospital she began going to nursery classes for normal children. She soon transferred to a special elementary school for handicapped children. Next, she spent several years in a city high school for the mentally retarded. Outside school, a speech therapist worked with her consistently for many years. Meanwhile, one of the therapists and his wife took Genie into their own home to live with their two teenage sons, a teenage daughter, a dog, and a cat. They tried to teach Genie to trace with her fingers the shape of sandpaper letters, to recognize words or work with Play-Doh, as well as deal with the demands of family life. She apparently had no trouble writing her name, and drew a number of pictures based on experiences she had had.

Nor did Genie's deficiencies appear to be inborn. Although many details of her early history are unclear, and Genie's mother had given contradictory accounts of them, Genie seems to have been a normal baby. She suffered from an Rh blood incompatibility, but received an exchange transfusion one day after birth. During her first year of life, before she was isolated from the rest of her family, she may have been on the road to language, since her mother reported that she heard Genie saying words right after she was locked up.

The gift of language has always been viewed as distinctively human, or even as proof of the existence of the soul. Its source has mystified human beings for millennia. In the 13th century, Frederick II, Emperor of the Holy Roman Empire, decided to perform an experiment to find out what kind of speech children would develop if left to their own devices in their early years; he wondered whether it would be Hebrew, Greek, Latin, or the language of their parents. He selected a few newborns and decreed that no one speak to them. The babies were suckled and bathed as usual, but songs and lullabies were strictly forbidden. Frederick II never got his answer, however, for the children all died. The experiment was never repeated.

In the early 19th century, Itard tried desperately to teach Victor, the wild boy of Aveyron, to speak. He began when Victor was about 12 years old—around the time of puberty, as with Genie. However, Victor never spoke more than a few single words, perhaps because of an injury to his throat, where he had a scar.

Chomsky believes that human beings are born with a unique competence for language, built into their brains. But he adds that the innate mechanisms that underlie this competence must be activated by exposure to language at the proper time, which Chomsky speculates must occur before puberty.

The strongest evidence that certain brain structures require triggering by the environment and that this triggering must occur during certain critical periods comes from research on the brains of cats. The visual centers of cats have very specific "feature detectors," cells that fire only in response to certain lines or angles. If a kitten is kept in a bare room lined only with vertical stripes for the period between its third week and third month of life and is then taken out, it will be able to see chair legs and other vertical objects without trouble but will act as if horizontal surfaces did not exist. By contrast, kittens that are kept in a room with only horizontal stripes during the same period will have no problem jumping from table to floor but will bump into table legs, as if vertical objects did not exist. At the Physiological Laboratory at Cambridge University in England, where this experiment was performed, Colin Blakemore placed electrodes in the cats' brains and discovered that each group of cats lacked a different set of feature detectors. In the visual cortex of cats that had seen only horizontal lines, no cells responded to vertical lines, while in the visual cortex of cats that had been exposed only to vertical lines, no cells responded to horizontal lines. The cells either had somehow failed to become functional or had atrophied from disuse.

Other animals also have critical periods of that sort. Thus, white-crowned sparrow chicks must hear their species' song between their 10th and 50th days of life, according to James L. Gould, a Princeton biology professor. Only during that period can they "tape" and store the parental songs in their brains, an essential step toward reproducing this song later in life. There is some evidence that such songs contain key sounds that automatically trigger the chicks' internal tape recorders to go on—and that those triggers consist of special feature detectors in the birds' brains.

Among human beings, four-week-old babies can recognize the difference between some 40 consonants that are used in human languages, as shown by how their sucking and heartbeats change when different consonant sounds are presented by audiotape. That ability seems to be innate, since babies respond to many more consonants than are used in their parents' language—English for example, has only 24 consonant sounds, yet babies of English-speaking parents react to the consonants present in Japanese. Babies lose that ability as they grow up. By the age of six, when children enter school, their ability to hear the difference between sounds to which they have not been exposed in their own language is severely reduced. Feature detectors responsible for recognizing about a dozen consonant sounds have so far been inferred to exist in the human brain. They need to be triggered by the environment, however: if not, they appear to atrophy.

Had something similar happened to Genie's brain? Curtiss raised that possibility when she reported that Genie, unlike 99 percent of righthanded people, seemed to use the right hemisphere of her brain for language. Since the left hemisphere is predisposed for language in righthanded people, that could account for some of the strange features of Genie's language development.

On tests of "dichotic listening," for example, which involve presenting different sounds to both ears simultaneously and asking the subject to react to them, "Genie's left ear outperformed her right ear on every occasion," Curtiss reports in her book. (Sound from the left ear is linked to the right hemisphere: from the right ear, to the left hemisphere.) Furthermore, "the degree of ear advantage is abnormal: Genie's left ear performed at 100 percent accuracy, while the right ear performed at a level below chance." That indicated Genie was using her right hemisphere as consistently as do people in whom, because of damage or surgery, only the right hemisphere is functioning.

When Genie's brain-wave patterns were examined at the UCLA Brain Research Institute—first as she listened to different sentences, then as she looked at pictures of faces—the data suggested that

Genie used her right hemisphere for both language and nonlanguage functions. Genie also proved to be particularly good at tasks involving the right hemisphere, such as recognizing faces. On the Mooney Faces Test, which requires the subject to distinguish real from "false" faces in which features are misplaced and to point out several features on each face, Genie's performance was "the highest reported in the literature for either child or adult," according to Curtiss.

From the very beginning, Genie's vocabulary revealed an extraordinary attention to the visual world, which is the special province of the right hemisphere—to color, shape, and size. All of her first two-word phrases were about static objects. While normal children usually start talking about people and actions or about the relations between people and objects, Genie spoke primarily about the attributes of things: "black shoe," "lot bread."

While summarizing the numerous tests made on Genie until 1979, Curtiss noted that Genie's performance had increased consistently over the years. For example, on the Leiter International Performance Scale, which was developed for use with deaf children and does not require verbal instructions, she had an IQ of 38 in 1971, an IQ of 53 in 1972, an IQ of 65 in 1974, and an IQ of 74 in 1977. However, she had made much less progress on tasks governed primarily by the left hemisphere. Even at the age of 20, she still performed at a three-year-old level on tests of auditory memory (a left-hemisphere task): she scored at a 6-to-12-year-old level on tests of visual memory (which tap both hemispheres), and at an adult level on tests of Gestalt perception (a right-hemisphere task).

The theory of language learning recently offered by Curtiss is an attempt to explain Genie's dependence on her right hemisphere. Possibly, Curtiss wrote in a paper on cognitive linguistics published by UCLA, the acquisition of language is what triggers the normal pattern of hemispheric specialization. Therefore, if language is not acquired at the appropriate time, "the cortical tissue normally committed for language and related abilities may functionally atrophy," Curtiss wrote. That would mean that there are critical periods for the development of the left hemisphere. If such development fails, later learning may be limited to the right hemisphere.

Researchers who have studied deaf children have found similar changes—in reverse—in the brain organization of children who learned sign language in infancy. Two groups of profoundly deaf children were tested at the Salk Institute in La Jolla, California, by Helen Neville. Members of one group could neither speak nor use sign language; when they were shown line drawings of common objects, there was no difference between the brain waves in their left and right hemispheres. The other group had had at least one deaf parent and had learned sign language in early childhood; they showed normal left-hemisphere specialization for language ability (in their case, that meant sign recognition), and their left hemisphere also appeared to be specialized for picture recognition, an ability that is normally confined to the right hemisphere. Based on these and other findings, Neville hypothesized that when any kind of language is acquired in childhood, it is lateralized to the left hemisphere (at least in right-handed people), and that the nature of the language system learned—whether it is auditory or visual—determines, in part, what else goes to the same hemisphere. Together, the two hypotheses present a new view of the development of the brain's hemispheres.

Obviously Genie has many problems besides her lack of syntax or her dependence on the right hemisphere of her brain. During her most formative years—her entire childhood—she was malnourished, abused, unloved, bereft of any toys or companionship. Naturally, she is strange in many ways. Yet her language deficits remain particularly striking since she often found means of explaining what was important to her. She used gestures if necessary (starting in 1974, she received regular lessons in American Sign Language to complement her spoken language). Once she wanted an egg-shaped container that held panty hose that was made of chrome-colored plastic. She signaled her desire by making the shape of an egg with her hands, and then pointing to many other things with a chromium finish.

In her book, Curtiss describes how Genie occasionally used her limited language to remember her past and to tell about details of her confinement. "Father hit arm. Big wood. Genie cry," she said once. Another time, when Curtiss took her into the city to browse through shops, Genie said, "Genie happy."

In 1978, Genie's mother became her legal guardian. During all the years of Genie's rehabilitation, her mother had also received help. An eye operation restored her sight, and a social worker tried to improve her behavior toward Genie. Genie's mother had never been held legally responsible for the child's inhuman treatment. Charges of child abuse were dismissed in 1970, when her lawyer argued that she "was, herself, a victim of the same psychotic individual"—her husband. There was "nothing to show purposeful or willful cruelty," he said.

Nevertheless, for many years the court assigned a guardian for Genie. Shortly after Genie's mother was named guardian, she astounded the therapists and researchers who had worked with Genie by filing a suit against Curtiss and the Children's Hospital among others—on behalf of herself and her daughter—in which she charged that they had disclosed private and confidential information concerning Genie and her mother for "prestige and profit" and had subjected Genie to "unreasonable and outrageous" testing, not for treatment, but to exploit Genie for personal and economic benefits. According to the *Los Angeles Times,* the lawyer who represents Genie's mother estimated that the actual damages could total $500,000.

The case has not yet come to court, but in the two years since it was filed, Genie has been completely cut off from the professionals at Children's Hospital and UCLA. Since she is too old to be in a foster home, she apparently is living in a board-and-care home for adults who cannot live alone. The *Los Angeles Times* reported that as of 1979 her mother was working as a domestic servant. All research on Genie's language and intellectual development has come to a halt. However, the research Genie stimulated goes on. Much of it concerns the relationship between linguistic ability and cognitive development, a subject to which Genie has made a significant contribution.

Apart from Chomsky and his followers, who believe that fundamental language ability is innate and unrelated to intelligence, most psychologists assume that the development of language is tied to—and emerges from—the development of nonverbal intelligence, as described by Piaget. However, Genie's obvious nonverbal intelligence—her use of tools, her drawings, her knowledge of causality, her mental maps of space—did not lead her to an equivalent competence in the grammar normal children acquire by the age of five.

Puzzled by the discrepancy between Genie's cognitive abilities and her language deficits, Curtiss and Fromkin wondered whether they could find people with the opposite pattern—who have normal language ability despite cognitive deficits. That would be further evidence of the independence of language from certain aspects of cognition.

In recent months, they have found several such persons among the mentally retarded, as well as among victims of Turner's syndrome, a chromosomal defect that produces short stature, cardiac problems, infertility, and specific learning difficulties in females. With help from the National Science Foundation (which had also funded some of Curtiss's research on Genie), Fromkin and Curtiss have identified and started working with some children and adolescents who combine normal grammatical ability with serious defects in logical reasoning, sequential ability, or other areas of thinking.

"You can't explain their unimpaired syntax on the basis of their impaired cognitive development," says Curtiss, who is greatly excited by this new developmental profile. She points out that in the youngsters studied, the purely grammatical aspect of language—which reflects Chomsky's language universals—seems to be isolated from the semantic aspect of language, which is more tied to cognition. "Language no longer looks like a uniform package," she declares. "This is the first experimental data on the subject." Thus the ordeal of an abused child may help us understand some of the most puzzling but important aspects of our humanity.

PART 2
Discussion Questions

1. How does the case of Genie support the notion that there is a critical period for language acquisition?
2. Even though she was discovered after the critical period for language development, Genie managed to acquire a few rudimentary language skills. Briefly describe the language skills Genie learned.
3. How does the case of Genie support the interactionist perspective on language acquisition?
4. What does Genie's language acquisition suggest about the lateralization of language in the brain?

Suggested Readings

Brown, R. (1973). *A first language: The early stages.* Cambridge, MA: Harvard University Press.

Rymer, R. (1993). *Genie.* New York: Harper Collins.

MODULE 14

LANGUAGE DEVELOPMENT

In this module, you will learn more about language development. You will analyze three transcriptions of mother-child conversations. Questions are provided to facilitate a discussion of this topic.

INTRODUCTION

Language development involves the understanding of various dimensions of language from phonology and morphology to semantics, syntax and pragmatics. Morphemes are the smallest unit of language that can change the meaning of a word. For example, apple and apples are words with notably different meanings due to the addition of the -s on the end of apples. Walk and walked refer to different actions due to the addition of -ed on the end of walk. One hallmark of language development is the acquisition of an increasingly sophisticated morphology (i.e., use of morphemes). Therefore, the average number of morphemes used in a sentence is a useful indicator of young children's language abilities. Psychologists measure this quantity and call it MLU or mean length utterance.

One way to get an appreciation of morphology is to learn to calculate MLU. Part 1 of this module provides three short transcripts of child language. Part 2 has a list of morphemes and instructions for calculating MLU. Part 3 is a set of questions to facilitate discussion of MLU and language development.

PART 1
TRANSCRIPTS

Child #1

Below is the transcript of a conversation between a mother and a child as they are playing with a toy telephone:

> M: What do you do with that?
> C: You push the buttons?
> M: Why do you push the buttons?

C:	They are not workin.
M:	They are not working? What are they doing to do with that? Are they hard to push?
C:	Yes.
M:	Why would you use a telephone?...Hmm, what do you do with a telephone?
C:	You, you talked in your ear.
M:	You talk with it in your ear. To whom do you talk?
C:	Nobody is talking.

Child #2

Below is the transcript of a conversation between a mother and child as they are playing with camping equipment:

M:	Let's pack up our bags so we can go camping. What are these?
C:	What are these? Hey, these are for your sandwich. Let's make a sandwich.
M:	Well, let's go fishing first and then we can make a sandwich. Is that okay?
C:	No. We can't. We have to make a sandwich right now.
M:	You want to put your potato chips on your sandwich?
C:	We need to put some mustard.
M:	Can you make Mommy a sandwich so I don't get hungry while you eat yours? What's that?
C:	A salami! (Mother hands child a slice of cheese.) It's cheese.

Child #3

Below is a transcription of a conversation between a mother and a child talking about a field trip:

C:	There is a maze and after we finished our lunch we could enter the maze and there are some dead ends and some people were playing tag.
M:	What is the maze made from?
C:	Well, the bottom is rocks and the um its like this um made out of this plastic stuff. Have you ever been on a trampoline? You know the outside,
M:	Yeah.
C:	It was kind of that stuff.
M:	Oh okay. So what happened?
C:	And before that we were at the butterfly house. That was the first thing we did. And then we went to, um, then we went to, to um, the reptile show. He showed a baby alligator.
M:	Wow, was it neat?
C:	Yeah and he showed us a snake and he showed a box turtle and he showed us an iguana. And we got to pet the snake and we got to take some snakeskin.
M:	Oh, neat.

PART 2
Coding MLU

The table below lists various types of morphemes. For each transcript, circle the morphemes and identify their form. MLU is calculated by adding up the number of morphemes and dividing by the total number of phrases.

Form	Meaning	Example
1. Present progressive: -ing	Ongoing process	He is sitting down.
2. Preposition: in	Containment	The mouse is in the box.
3. Preposition: on	Support	The book is on the table.
4. Plural: -s	Number	The dogs ran away.
5. Past irregular: e.g., went	Earlier in time relative to time speaking	The boy went home.
6. Possessive: 's	Possession	The girl's dog is big.
7. Uncontractible copula be: are, was	Number; earlier in time	Are they boys or girls?
8. Articles: the, a	Definite/indefinite	He has a book.
9. Past regular: -ed	Earlier in time	He jumped the stream.
10. Third person regular: -s	Number; earlier in time	She runs fast.
11. Third person irregular: has, done	Number; earlier in time	Does the dog bark?
12. Uncontractible auxillary: is, were	Number; earlier in time; ongoing process	Were they at home? Is he running?
13. Contractible copula be: 's, 're	Number; earlier in time	That's a spaniel.
14. Contractible auxillary be: 's, 're	Number; earlier in time; ongoing process	They're running very slowly.

PART 3
Discussion Questions

1. Research has shown that children tend to acquire grammatical rules in a consistent order. What is the highest level of performance displayed by each child? Is this related to the child's age?

2. Other aspects of language are also interesting. Count the number of times the child used any of the following advanced structures: past tense, adjectives, personal pronouns.

3. The child's errors can be informative. Make a list of any errors the child makes that could be considered overextension (i.e., using a word more broadly than would be considered correct by an adult speaker), underextension (i.e., using a word too narrowly), or over-regularization (i.e., applying a grammatical rule in a context in which it should not be used, such as *we goed to the movie*).

4. Note any examples of the adults' efforts to scaffold or support the child's language (e.g., reinforcement, imitation, expansion, or recasting).

MODULE 15

DEVELOPMENTALLY APPROPRIATE CHILDREN'S LITERATURE AND FILM

Children's literature and film are a ready source for examples of how children think and feel. This module will prompt you to examine more closely the books and movies produced for children and to identify instances of developmental constructs as portrayed in these media. Questions are provided to facilitate discussion of this topic.

■ INTRODUCTION

It might be argued that children's books and films become popular in part because of their ability to engage children on their own cognitive or emotional levels. In this way, children are able to identify with the characters in the story and understand their reactions to the situations they face. Children of different ages appreciate different forms of humor and can cope with different levels of surprise and fear. By the same token, when a book or movie fails to reach children in a developmentally appropriate manner, they may find it uninteresting or even confusing or disturbing.

Part 1 of this module offers examples of how developmental constructs can be identified in popular children's literature and film. Part 2 of the module asks you to select a children's book or film and identify aspects of the work that would appeal to children of particular ages and the developmental constructs that they exemplify. Part 3 of the module poses questions to facilitate a discussion of this topic.

PART 1
■ DEVELOPMENTAL CONSTRUCTS IN POPULAR CHILDREN'S LITERATURE AND FILM

Here are two illustrations of how developmentally appropriate thought and feelings are embodied in children's literature and film:

The first example comes from the Walt Disney film *Bambi*. The scene in which the young deer Bambi and his rabbit friend Thumper are frolicking in the woods and Bambi is learning the names of things offers a clear illustration of the processes of assimilation and accommodation. First, Bambi learns what a bird is. Then, he mistakenly identifies a butterfly as a bird because it flies—assimilation. When Thumper corrects him and Bambi correctly identifies a butterfly, accommodation has taken place. Next, Bambi misidentifies a flower as a butterfly because of their similarity in shape and color—again, assimilation. Accommodation follows as he learns that flowers are different from butterflies.

A second series of examples can be found in *Winnie the Pooh* by A. A. Milne. The Pooh stories on the whole can be viewed as representations of animistic thinking because most of the characters in them are in fact stuffed animals belonging to Christopher Robin. In one chapter of the book, Pooh and other inhabitants of the Hundred Acre Wood learn that Eeyore the donkey is celebrating a birthday. Each of his friends tries to find a gift for him. Upon brief reflection, being "a bear of very little brains," Pooh decides to take Eeyore a small pot of honey. After all, Pooh himself would enjoy receiving such a gift—egocentrism. Piglet chooses to give Eeyore a balloon, but on his way to deliver the gift, he trips and bursts it. He presents the remnants to Eeyore who asks what color they were when they were a balloon, as if the change in state had changed other essential properties—lack of conservation.

As you may have noticed, the examples provided here focus on Piagetian concepts, but other constructs and developmental processes can be identified in these and other works for children. For example, in the Pooh stories, language is manipulated in a way to highlight some of the difficulties young children have with pronunciation. "Tiger" becomes "Tigger," and "elephants and weasels" become "heffalumps and woozels." Similarly, aspects of peer relations and friendship formation figure prominently in *Ramona the Pest* and other books by Beverly Cleary.

PART 2
■ CHOOSE A BOOK OR A FILM TO EXAMINE

Select a children's book to read or film to watch. Record the title, author/producer, and approximate target age level of the work. Take note of any developmental constructs that you are able to identify in the work.

PART 3
■ DISCUSSION QUESTIONS

1. To what extent do you think children's authors/filmmakers intentionally and explicitly consider developmental issues in creating their works? Do you think such concerns are more evident in certain books/films?
2. To what extent do you think children realize that characters in books and movies think and feel like they do? Do they realize that the stories are sometimes designed this way?

3. Think back to your own childhood. What books and films were your favorites? Why did you like them? With your current level of understanding, can you offer developmental reasons for your choices?
4. Do you think some developmental issues are easier to address than others in books and films?
5. What consequences might exposure to developmentally appropriate entertainment have? Can you think of possible negative effects? What consequences might exposure to developmentally inappropriate entertainment have?
6. The focus in this module has been on fictional literature and films. What efforts do you think are made by authors of nonfiction books for children to be developmentally appropriate?

MODULE 16

CHILDREN AS EYEWITNESSES

This module addresses the topic of children testifying in courts of law about alleged criminal events they have witnessed, as well as crimes in which they were the direct victims. The cognitive and social skills of child witnesses are different from those of adults, and forensic interviewers must be sensitive to the level of children's abilities to provide testimony. It is necessary that such interviewers adjust their approach while questioning them, so as to not compromise the reliability of the testimony. You will be presented with a number of vignettes stemming from different transcripts of children's testimony. Based on your reading of these transcripts, you will be asked to identify aspects of interviewing techniques that might prove problematic, given young children's cognitive and social skills. In a final step, you will be asked to summarize your ideas in the form of recommendations for adequate interviewing practice.

▎INTRODUCTION

Over the past two decades, young children have increasingly been called upon to testify as witnesses in courts of law. The testimony that these children provide can in some instances be crucial to the outcome of the case, especially in cases where a child is the only witness to the alleged crime. This may be particularly true for cases of sexual abuse. It has therefore been a concern of much applied research to understand the factors that influence the quality of children's testimony.

Providing testimony is a very complex task that requires many different cognitive and social skills. At a minimum, the statements that a child can make about events that have occurred in the past rely heavily on his or her memory. An enormous amount of developmental research has shown that young children may not be as proficient at committing information to and later retrieving it from memory than older children and adults. But developmental differences extend beyond the realm of memory, *per se*. Giving testimony also involves a variety of other aspects, such as correctly understanding and interpreting the questions that are asked by professionals in the legal arena (e.g., prosecutors), as well as formulating accurate and coherent verbal accounts of the information that is remembered. Furthermore, being on the witness stand is also a profoundly social situation that involves other actors and their respective agendas. These social issues may also affect the performance of a witness.

Some of the cognitive and social skills that are involved when providing eyewitness testimony in court may not yet be fully developed in young children. Much proficiency is therefore needed on the part of the interviewer to elicit useful and reliable information through questions. The interviewing process thus becomes a crucial factor for the quality of testimony. Below, you will find some examples from actual interview transcripts. These examples were chosen to highlight particular aspects of the interviewing techniques that are commonly used when questioning child witnesses about events in the past. It will be your task to identify potential problems in how the interviewers go about obtaining information from the children.

After working through the specific examples, you will be asked to think of ways to avoid the mistakes these interviewers have made by summarizing your findings in the form of a recommendation of good interviewing techniques.

PART 1
Examples and Questions

Example 1

A four-year-old witness was asked during questioning, "On the evening of January third, you did, didn't you, visit your grandmother's sister's house and didn't you see the defendant leave the house at 7:30, after which you stayed the night?" The child sat in silence and became tearful (Saywitz & Snyder, 1993, p. 117).

Questions for Example 1
1. In what way(s) might the interviewer's question be inappropriate?
2. What is the interviewer implicitly assuming about the child's abilities?
3. What might the interviewer do differently in order to obtain the pertinent information from the four-year-old?

Example 2

Interviewer: Tell me everything you can remember.
Child: They took his money.
Interviewer: Is there anything else that you can remember? Everything is important, even details.
Child: They took off on their bikes. That was mean.
(translated from Roebers & Elischberger, 2002, p. 2).

Questions for Example 2
1. As the above example illustrates, young children may not provide extensive amounts of information when asked rather general questions (e.g., who is "they"?). What could you do as an interviewer to obtain more specific information from the child witness?
2. Can you see any potential problems with the approaches you suggested?

Example 3

The following illustrates that an interviewer's assumptions regarding children's legal vocabulary may not be justified:

Here are some of the answers that younger children gave when asked to define "jury":

- "Jury is that stuff my mom wears around her neck and fingers."
- "A trip" (journey).

Similarly, 5- and 6-year-olds may define legal terms exclusively in familiar non-legal terms, such as

- "Court": "Court is a place to play basketball."
- "Hearing": "A hearing is something you do with your ears."
- "Charges": "Charges are something you do with credit cards."

Questions for Example 3

1. What problems do these examples highlight?
2. What are potential consequences for a child's testimony if this problem is not recognized and properly dealt with?
3. How would you try to resolve this issue?

Example 4

The following example is of an exchange between a child witness in the "Little Rascals" case and the prosecuting attorney (Ceci & Bruck, 1993, p. 121):

> Prosecuting Attorney: And when you were laying on top of Bridget, where was your private?
> Child: I forgot.
> Prosecuting Attorney: Do you remember telling Mrs. Judy that you had to put your private next to her private? Did you have to do that, (child's name)?
> Child: No Sir.
> Prosecuting Attorney: What did you say?
> Child: No Sir.
> Prosecuting Attorney: Did you say No or Yes?
> Child: Yes Sir.

Questions for Example 4

1. Would you take the child's answer to be a Yes or a No? What can be considered problematic with this form of interviewing style?
2. How might this type of questioning influence the child's report?
3. Do you believe that the information provided by the child is reliable?

Example 5

The following example is of an exchange between an interviewer and a child involved in the Country Walk case (Ceci & Bruck, 1993, p. 136):

> Child: I am afraid of them [Frank and Iliana] now because my mom told me that they are strangers.
> Interviewer: Were you afraid of them before?

Child: (Nodding in the negative).
Interviewer: No? You only...

Questions for Example 5
1. What social processes seem to have influenced this child's testimony?
2. What may be the consequences of the mother's actions to the child's memory?

Example 6

Sometimes anatomically detailed dolls are used in interviewing children about events involving their own bodies. This is done in part to help them overcome verbal limitations. The following example is a mother's report of her eavesdropping on her child's doll-centered interview (Ceci & Bruck, 1993, p. 175):

> Mother: I couldn't see what was going on, but at some point the dolls came out. I remember clearly hearing [the interviewer] saying, "You do realize the difference between little boys and little girls, and little boys have a penis and little girls have an opening here."

Questions for Example 6
1. As this example illustrates, the interviewer might in some cases introduce information (e.g., about physical differences between boys and girls) that is new to the child. Even if the genital information itself is not new, it is very likely that the child has not had prior contact with anatomically detailed dolls. What potential dangers do you see in using such novel props when interviewing young children? What are potential advantages of using dolls to interview children?
2. What skills must the child have in order to use the dolls to report about something that involved their own bodies?

Example 7

The following is a statement made by a police officer prior to interviewing a child (Ceci & Bruck, 1993, p. 152):

> Police Officer: I'm a policeman, if you were a bad girl, I would punish you wouldn't I? Police can punish bad people.

Questions for Example 7
1. What are some contextual factors that may influence the children's reports? For example, do you think it might make a difference to a child whether she is interviewed by a policeman in uniform rather than civilian clothing?
2. What other contextual factors might be important?
3. How might the child respond to these contextual factors?

PART 2
GENERAL DISCUSSION QUESTIONS

1. After reading the examples listed above, what are some general guidelines that you would suggest to interviewers about obtaining information from children?
2. If you were a jury member, and a key piece of the prosecution's case proving guilt relied on a child's testimony, what information would you want to know about the child's eyewitness report?

SUGGESTED READING

Bruck, M. & Ceci, S. J. (1997). The description of children's suggestibility. In N. L. Stein, P. A. Ornstein, B. Tversky & C. Brainerd (Eds.), *Memory for everyday and emotional events* (pp. 371–400). Mahwah, NJ: Erlbaum.

Ceci, S. J., & Bruck, M. (1995). *Jeopardy in the courtroom: A scientific analysis of children's testimony.* Washington, DC: American Psychological Association.

Roebers, C. M., & Elischberger, H. B. (2002). Autobiographische Erinnerung bei jungen Kindern: Möglichkeiten und Grenzen bei der Verbesserung ihrer freien Berichte. *Zeitschrift für Entwicklungspsychologie und Pädagogische Psychologie, 34 (1),* 2–10. [Young children's autobiographical memory: Methods to improve their free narratives and limitations. *Journal of Developmental Psychology and Pedagogical Psychology.*]

Saywitz, K. J. (1995). Improving children's testimony. The question, the answer, and the environment. In M. S. Zaragoza, J. R. Graham, G. C. N. Hall, R. Hirschman & Y. S. Ben-Porath (Eds.), *Memory and testimony in the child witness* (pp. 113–139). Thousand Oaks: Sage.

Saywitz, K. J. & Snyder, L. (1993). Improving children's testimony with preparation. In G. S. Goodman & B. L. Bottoms (Eds.), *Child victims, child witnesses. understanding and improving testimony* (pp. 117–146). New York: Guilford Press.

MODULE 17

SOCIOMETRY AND SOCIAL NETWORKING

Considerable research has documented the substantial impact of peer influence on human behavior and development. Peer socialization affects children even as early as the preschool years, and becomes even more important in adolescence and young adulthood. In current literature, two distinct traditions have emerged whereby information on the peer group is used to study individual social development. The first consists of using peers to derive measures of likeability and rejection and the second consists of mapping out the groups of which the individual is a member. As you will see, these two methods provide very distinct types of information. In this module you will be asked to contrast the two methods and to discuss how the information they yield may be used to study social development.

PART 1
SOCIOMETRIC STATUS

Sociometric status is determined by peer nomination. Children are asked to answer questions such as "Whom do you like most? [i.e., in your class]" and "Whom do you like least?". Using these scores, researchers are able to create two dimensions for every child in the class: social preference and social impact. Social preference is a proxy for how popular a child is, while social impact is a proxy for how salient, both positively and negatively, a child is in the mind of his or her peers. The two dimensions are calculated as follows:

Social Preference = # Likes most votes – # Likes least votes
Social Impact = # Likes most votes + # Likes least votes

These dimensions allow researchers to classify children into 1 of 5 categories of sociometric status.

1. Popular: high is social preference, high in social impact
2. Rejected: low in social preference, low to moderate in social impact
3. Controversial: high in social impact, moderate in social preference
4. Neglected: low in social impact, low in social preference
5. Average: moderate in social impact and social preference

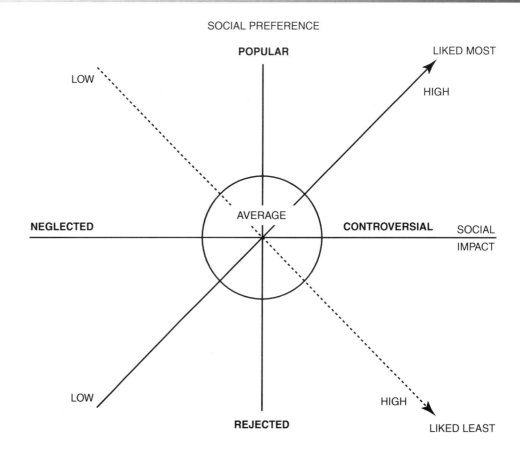

PART 2
Social Networks

Although sociometric status data provide interesting information on the individual (as perceived by the group), it does not provide detailed information about the group itself. For instance, an individual may be categorized as popular by means of sociometric nomination, but that tells us nothing of *who* his friends are or of the intimacy of those relationships. This information is crucial for understanding the processes by which social experiences shape behavior. For instance, both rejection and popularity could be linked to aggression; it is the knowledge of group composition and dynamics that discriminates alternative pathways for such shared behavior.

How are social networks created? The most direct way to gather information about peer groups is to go to the source. Because children are often aware of more peer dynamics than they actually experience, simply asking children a few select questions can be a rich and efficient source of data. For instance, children can be asked:

"Are there people in school who hang around together a lot? Who are they? (If only same-sex groups were named, children [are] asked:) Are there any groups of boys/girls? (If the subject himself/herself was not included, he/she was asked:) What about yourself? Do you have a group you hang around with in

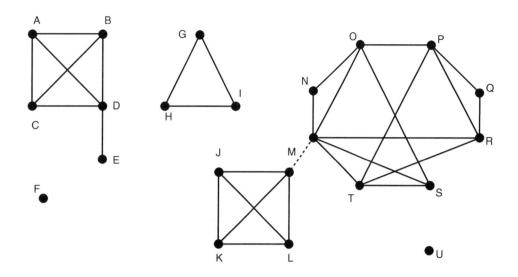

school? What about outside of school, do you have a group you hang around with?" (Cairns & Cairns, 1994, p. 101)

Using this information, social networks such as the following can be created, using lines to indicate friendships between individuals:

As you can see, this kind of data provides information on both how many friends a child has, who these friends are, and how central they are in the peer group.

PART 3
■ Exercise on Sociometry and Social Networking

After familiarizing yourself with both methods, try to think back to the days of middle and high school. Read the following individual descriptions and predict how they may be categorized according to sociometric status and where they would fall in the social network illustrated above.

1. Ron is one of the best athletes in school. He has a close group of friends that are all varsity athletes, and many people try to emulate him. Most of the girls would love to date him, although he only pays attention to a select few. In addition, he has been known to be a bit of a bully, but only by making fun of others, never by fighting.
2. Daniel is one of the smartest students in the school, and although he has a few friends he tends to stick mostly to himself. He tutors several people after school, and has positive relations with most of the people in his class. Despite his intelligence and moderate athletic ability, he does not participate in any academic or athletic extracurricular activities.
3. Donna is attractive and athletic, but does not participate in class or in any extracurricular activities. She has a large group of friends at school, but rarely hangs out with them outside of school hours. At lunch she often sits with a large group of people, although she rarely speaks.

4. Brad is two years older than the rest of the class. Although he is physically more mature, he is not the smartest. Many of the girls in the class pay a lot of attention to him, but he has relatively few male friends. He tends to pick fights with others, which he often wins, given his size.

5. Joanna is a smart and attractive but purposely wears clothes and exhibits behaviors that are designed to shock her peers and teachers. Although she performs well at school, she tends to be confrontational with adults and dismissive with peers. Several students in the class respect her audacity and in-your-face sense of humor, but few ever invite her to join them for lunch.

Discuss your decisions with the class. Did everyone agree on where the people would fall sociometrically or within the social network? After comparing placements, to what extent do agreements and disagreements illustrate the strengths and weaknesses of each method?

PART 4
Discussion Questions

1. How do the types of information produced from each method of analysis differ? (Think in terms of analyzing the individual versus the group and the subsequent utility and domain-specific [i.e., education, clinical intervention, etc.] value of the information you gather).
2. Is it possible for sociometrically rejected individual to be well-integrated members of a social network?
3. Could sociometric ratings be used to predict who will affiliate with whom?
4. On the basis of information on social network composition, could you take the further step of identifying the influences that may be affecting its members?
5. How does social membership contribute to consolidate individual characteristics and favor continuity in social development?

Selected Readings

Asher, S. R., & Hymel, S. (1981). Children's social competence in peer relations: Sociometric and behavioral assessment. In J. D. Wine & M. D. Syme (Eds.), *Social competence.* New York: Guilford.

Bergman, L. R. (1998). A pattern-oriented approach for studying individual development. In R. B. Cairns, L. R. Bergman, & J. Kagan (Eds.), *Methods and models for studying the individual: Essays in honor of Marian Radke-Yarrow.* Thousand Oaks, CA: Sage.

Cairns, R. B. & Cairns, B. D. (1994). *Lifelines and risks: Pathways of youth in our time.* Hemel Hempstead (UK): Harvester Wheatsheaf and New York: Cambridge University Press.

Cairns, R. B., Xie, H., & Leung, M.-C. (1998). The popularity of friendship and the neglect of social networks: Toward a new balance. In W. M. Bukowski & A. H. Cilessen (Eds.), *Sociometry then and now: Building on six decades of measuring children's experiences with the peer group.* San Francisco: Jossey-Bass.

Coie, J. D., Dodge, K. A., & Coppotelli, H. (1982). Dimensions and types of social status: A cross-age perspective. *Developmental Psychology, 18,* 557–570.

MODULE 18

SEX DIFFERENCES

Males and females differ by virtue of their respective biological roles in reproduction, but they also differ in their behaviors. Although our own experience tells us that men and women behave differently, curiously, it has been rather difficult for psychologists to pinpoint exactly what the differences are. In this module you are invited to revisit the question, first by reading an article published by Maccoby, a researcher well known for her work on this topic, and then by discussing some questions about the article and the topic.

■ INTRODUCTION

In 1974, Maccoby and Jacklin published through Stanford University Press a book titled *The Psychology of Sex Differences* in which they summarized research on the question of behavioral differences between the sexes. Since then, this book has served as a major reference on the subject and virtually every textbook in psychology has cited it and used it to introduce the topic to psychology students. Yet, in the more recent article you are about to read, Maccoby comments that she and her co-author Jacklin "... felt at the time that the yield was thin. That is, there were very few attributes on which the average values for the two sexes differed consistently" (Maccoby, 1990, p. 513).

To put their feelings in context, here is what the authors reported back in 1974:

1. Males are more active than females.
2. Males are physically and verbally more aggressive than females.
3. Females show more emotional sensitivity and are more expressive; they are also more fearful and more timid than males.
4. Females are better than males on verbal abilities and males are better on visual/spatial abilities.
5. By adolescence (but not before), males are better in mathematics than females.

As you can see the yield was indeed "thin." Moreover, Maccoby and Jacklin (1974) also reported that these differences, except for physical and verbal aggression, were problematic because they: (1) were small in magnitude, (2) showed large intra-sex variability, (3) were not found in all cultures, and (4) often depended on socialization pressures.

In her more recent article, *Gender and Relationships*, Maccoby (1990) now argues that the failure to find more, and more consistent sex differences was attributable to the fact that they had only looked at individual, non-social, behaviors. By focusing on social variables, Maccoby's new list of sex differences in behavior is now more imposing. In Part 1 of this module we have reproduced this article for you to read. In Part 2, we ask that you construct a list of the sex differences reported by the author. Finally, in Part 3 we suggest a number of discussion questions that will ask you to evaluate the relative merits and limits of Maccoby's reanalysis of the question.

PART 1
REQUIRED READING

GENDER AND RELATIONSHIPS
A DEVELOPMENTAL ACCOUNT

Eleanor E. Maccoby *Stanford University*

From American Psychologist, *46, 1990 by E. Maccoby. Copyright © 1990 by the American Psychological Association. Reprinted with permission.*

ABSTRACT: This article argues that behavioral differentiation of the sexes is minimal when children are observed or tested individually. Sex differences emerge primarily in social situations, and their nature varies with the gender composition of dyads and groups. Children find same-sex play partners more compatible, and they segregate themselves into same-sex groups, in which distinctive interaction styles emerge. These styles are described. As children move into adolescence, the patterns they developed in their childhood same-sex groups are carried over into cross-sex encounters in which girls' styles put them at a disadvantage. Patterns of mutual influence can become more symmetrical in intimate male-female dyads, but the distinctive styles of the two sexes can still be seen in such dyads and are subsequently manifested in the roles and relationships of parenthood. The implications of these continuities are considered.

Historically, the way we psychologists think about the psychology of gender has grown out of our thinking about individual differences. We are accustomed to assessing a wide variety of attributes and skills and giving scores to individuals based on their standing relative to other individuals in a sample population. On most psychological attributes, we see wide variation among individuals, and a major focus of research has been the effort to identify correlates or sources of this variation. Commonly, what we have done is to classify individuals by some antecedent variable, such as age or some aspect of their environment, to determine how much of the variance among individuals in their performance on a given task can be accounted for by this so-called *antecedent* or *independent* variable. Despite the fact that hermaphrodites exist, almost every individual is either clearly male or clearly female. What could be more natural for psychologists than to ask how much variance among individuals is accounted for by this beautifully binary factor?

Fifteen years ago, Carol Jacklin and I put out a book summarizing the work on sex differences that had come out of the individual differences perspective (Maccoby & Jacklin, 1974). We felt at that time that the yield was thin. That is, there were very few attributes on which the average values for the two sexes differed consistently. Furthermore, even when consistent differences were found, the amount of variance accounted for by sex was small, relative to the amount of variation within each sex. Our conclusions fitted in quite well with the feminist zeitgeist of the times, when most feminists were taking a minimalist position, urging that the two sexes were basically alike and that any differences were either illusions in the eye of the beholder or reversible outcomes of social shaping. Our conclusions were challenged as having both overstated the case for sex differences (Tieger, 1980) and for having understated it (Block, 1976).

In the last 15 years, work on sex differences has become more methodologically sophisticated, with greater use of meta analyses to reveal not only the direction of sex differences but quantitative estimates of their magnitude. In my judgment, the conclusions are still quite similar to those Jacklin and I arrived at in 1974: There are still some replicable sex differences, of moderate magnitude, in performance on tests of mathematical and spatial abilities, although sex differences in verbal abilities have faded. Other aspects of intellectual performance continue to show gender equality. When it comes to attributes in the personality-social domain, results are particularly sparse and inconsistent. Studies continue to find that men are more often agents of aggression than are women (Eagly, 1987: Huston, 1985: Maccoby & Jacklin, 1980). Eagly (1983, 1987) reported in addition that women are more easily influenced than men and that men are more altruistic in the sense that they are more likely to offer help to others. In general, however, personality traits measured as characteristics of individuals do not appear to differ systematically by sex (Huston, 1985). This no doubt reflects in part the fact that male and female persons really are much alike, and their lives are governed mainly by the attributes that all persons in a given culture have in common. Nevertheless, I believe that the null findings coming out of comparisons of male and female individuals on personality measures are partly illusory. That is, they are an artifact of our historical reliance on an individual differences perspective. Social behavior, as many have pointed out, is never a function of the individual alone. It is a function of the interaction between two or more persons. Individuals behave differently with different partners. There are certain important ways in which gender is implicated in social behavior— ways that may be obscured or missed altogether when behavior is summed across all categories of social partners.

An illustration is found in a study of social interaction between previously unacquainted pairs of young children (mean age, 33 months; Jacklin & Maccoby, 1978). In some pairs, the children had same-sex play partners; in others, the pair was made up of a boy and a girl. Observers recorded the social behavior of each child on a time-sampling basis. Each child received a score for total social behavior directed toward the partner. This score included both positive and negative behaviors (e.g., offering a toy and grabbing a toy; hugging and pushing; vocally greeting, inviting, protesting, or prohibiting). There was no overall sex difference in the amount of social behavior when this was evaluated without regard to sex of partner. But there was a powerful interaction between sex of the subject and that of the partner: Children of each sex had much higher levels of social behavior when playing with a same-sex partner than when playing with a child of the other sex. This result is consistent with the findings of Wasserman and Stern (1978) that when asked to approach another child, children as young as age three stopped farther away when the other child was of the opposite sex, indicating awareness of gender similarity or difference, and wariness toward the other sex.

The number of time intervals during which a child was simply standing passively watching the partner play with the toys was also scored. There was no overall sex difference in the frequency of this behavior, but the behavior of girls was greatly affected by the sex of the partner. With other girls, passive behavior seldom occurred; indeed, in girl-girl pairs it occurred less often than it did in boy-boy pairs. However when paired with boys, girls frequently stood on the sidelines and let the boys monopolize the toys. Clearly, the little girls in this study were not more passive than the little boys in any overall, trait-like sense. Passivity in these girls could be understood only in relation to the characteristics of their interactive partners. It was a characteristic of girls in cross-sex dyads. This conclusion may not seem especially novel because for many years we have known that social behavior is situationally specific. However, the point here is that interactive behavior is not just situationally specific, but that it depends on the gender category membership of the participants. We can account for a good deal more of the behavior if we know the gender mix of dyads, and this probably holds true for larger groups as well.

An implication of our results was that if children at this early age found same-sex play partners more compatible, they ought to prefer same-sex partners when they entered group settings that included children of both sexes. There were already many indications in the literature that children do have same-sex playmate preferences, but there clearly was a need for more systematic attention to the degree of sex segregation that prevails in naturally occurring children's groups at different ages. As part of a longitudinal study of children from birth to age six, Jacklin and I did time-sampled behavioral observation of approximately 100 children on their preschool playgrounds, and again two years later when the children were playing during school recess periods (Maccoby & Jacklin, 1987). Same-sex playmate preference was clearly apparent in preschool when the children were approximately 4-1/2. At this age, the children were spending nearly 3 times as much time with same-sex play partners as with children of the other sex. By age 6-1/2, the preference had grown much stronger. At this time, the children were spending 11 times as much time with same-sex as with opposite-sex partners.

Elsewhere we have reviewed the literature on playmate choices (Maccoby, 1988; Maccoby & Jacklin, 1987), and here I will simply summarize what I believe the existing body of research shows:

1. Gender segregation is a widespread phenomenon. It is found in all the cultural settings in which children are in social groups large enough to permit choice.

2. The sex difference in the gender of preferred playmates is large in absolute magnitude, compared to sex differences found when children are observed or tested in nonsocial situations.

3. In a few instances, attempts have been made to break down children's preferences for interacting with other same-sex children. It has been found that the preferences are difficult to change.

4. Children choose same-sex playmates spontaneously in situations in which they are not under pressure from adults to do so. In modern co-educational schools, segregation is more marked in situations that have not been structured by adults than in those that have (e.g., Eisenhart & Holland, 1983). Segregation is situationally specific, and the two sexes can interact comfortably under certain conditions, for example, in an absorbing joint task, when structures and roles are set up by adults, or in non-public settings (Thorne, 1986).

5. Gender segregation is not closely linked to involvement in sex-typed activities. Preschool children spend a great deal of their time engaged in activities that are gender neutral, and segregation prevails in these activities as well as when they are playing with dolls or trucks.

6. Tendencies to prefer same-sex playmates can be seen among three-year-olds and at even earlier ages under some conditions. But the preferences increase in strength between preschool and school and are maintained at a high level between the ages of 6 and at least age 11.

7. The research base is thin, but so far it appears that a child's tendency to prefer same-sex playmates has little to do with that child's standing on measures of individual differences. In particular, it appears to be unrelated to measures of masculinity or femininity and also to measures of gender schematicity (Powlishta, 1989).

Why do we see such pronounced attraction to same-sex peers and avoidance of other-sex peers in childhood? Elsewhere I have summarized evidence pointing to two factors that seem to be important in the preschool years (Maccoby, 1988). The first is the rough-and-tumble play style characteristic of boys and their orientation toward issues of competition and dominance. These aspects of male-male interaction appear to be somewhat aversive to most girls. At least, girls are made wary by male play styles. The second factor of importance is that girls find it difficult to influence boys. Some important work by Serbin and colleagues (Serbin, Sprafkin, Elman, & Doyle, 1984) indicates that between the ages of 3-1/2 and 5-1/2, children greatly increase the frequency of their attempts to influence their play partners. This indicates that children are learning to integrate their activities with those of others so as to be able to carry out coordinated activities. Serbin and colleagues found that the increase in influence attempts by girls was almost entirely an increase in making polite suggestions to others, whereas among boys the increase took the form of more use of direct demands. Furthermore, during this formative two-year period just before school entry, boys were becoming less and less responsive to polite suggestions, so that the style being progressively adopted by girls was progressively less effective with boys. Girls' influence style was effective with each other and was well adapted to interaction with teachers and other adults.

These asymmetries in influence patterns were presaged in our study with 33-month-old children: We found then that boys were unresponsive to the vocal prohibitions of female partner (in that they did not withdraw), although they would respond when a vocal prohibition was issued by a male partner. Girls were responsive to one another and to a male partner's prohibitions. Fagot (1985) also reported that boys are "reinforced" by the reactions of male peers—in the sense that they modify their behavior following a male peer's reaction—but that their behavior appears not to be affected by a female's response.

My hypothesis is that girls find it aversive to try to interact with someone who is unresponsive and that they begin to avoid such partners. Students of power and bargaining have long been aware of the importance of reciprocity in human relations. Pruitt (1976) said, "Influence and power are omnipresent in human affairs. Indeed, groups cannot possibly function unless their members can influence one another" (p. 343). From this standpoint, it becomes clear why boys and girls have difficulty forming groups that include children of both sexes.

Why do little boys not accept influence from little girls? Psychologists almost automatically look to the nuclear family for the origins of behavior patterns seen in young children. It is plausible that boys may have been more reinforced for power assertive behavior by their parents, and girls more for politeness, although the evidence for such differential socialization pressure has proved difficult to come by. However, it is less easy to imagine how or why parents should reinforce boys for being unresponsive to *girls*. Perhaps it is a matter of observational learning: Children may have observed that between their two parents, their fathers are more influential than their mothers. I am skeptical about such an explanation. In the first place, mothers exercise a good deal of managerial authority within the households in which children live, and it is common for fathers to defer to their judgment in matters concerning the children: Or, parents form a coalition, and in the eyes of the children they become a joint authority, so that it makes little difference to them whether it is a mother or a father who is wielding authority at any given time. Furthermore, the asymmetry in children's cross-sex influence with their peers appears to have its origins at quite an early age—earlier, I would suggest, than children have a very clear idea about the connection between their own sex and that of the same-sex parent. In other words, it seems quite unlikely that little boys ignore girls' influence attempts because little girls remind them of their mothers. I think we simply do not know why girls' influence styles are ineffective with boys, but the fact that they are has important implications for a variety of social behaviors, not just for segregation.

Here are some examples from recent studies. Powlishta (1987) observed preschool-aged boy–girl pairs competing for a scarce resource. The children were brought to a playroom in the nursery school and were given an opportunity to watch cartoons through a movie-viewer that could only be accessed by one child at a time. Powlishta found that when the two children were alone together in the playroom, the boys got more than their share of access to the movie-viewer. When there was an adult present, however, this was no longer the case. The adult's presence appeared to inhibit the boys' more power-assertive techniques and resulted in girls having at least equal access.

This study points to a reason why girls may not only avoid playing with boys but may also stay nearer to a teacher or other adult. Following up on this possibility, Greeno (1989) brought four-child groups of kindergarten and first-grade children into a large playroom equipped with attractive toys. Some of the quartets were all-boy groups, some all-girl groups, and some were made up of two boys and two girls. A female adult sat at one end of the room, and halfway through the play session, moved to a seat at the other end of the room. The question posed for this study was: Would girls move closer to the teacher when boys were present than when they were not? Would the sex composition of a play group make any difference to the locations taken up by the boys? The results were that in all-girl groups, girls actually took up locations *farther* from the adult than did boys in all-boy groups. When two boys were present, however, the two girls were significantly closer to the adult than were the boys, who tended to remain at intermediate distances. When the adult changed position halfway through the session, boys' locations did not change, and this was true whether there were girls present or not. Girls in all-girl groups tended to move in the opposite direction when the adult moved; maintaining distance between themselves and the adult; when boys were present, however, the girls tended to move *with* the adult, staying relatively close. It is worth noting, incidentally, that in all the mixed-sex groups except one, segregation was extreme; both boys and girls behaved as though there was only one playmate available to them, rather than three.

There are some fairly far-reaching implications of this study. Previous observational studies in preschools had indicated that girls are often found in locations closer to the teacher than are boys. These studies have been done in mixed-sex nursery school groups. Girls' proximity seeking toward adults has often been interpreted as a reflection of some general affiliative trait in girls and perhaps as a reflection of some aspect of early socialization that has bound them more closely to caregivers. We see in the Greeno study that proximity seeking toward adults was *not* a general trait in girls. It was a function of the gender composition of the group of other children present as potential interaction partners. The behavior of girls implied that they found the presence of boys to be less aversive when an adult was nearby. It was as though they realized that the rough, power-assertive behavior of boys was likely to be moderated in the presence of adults, and indeed, there is evidence that they were right.

We have been exploring some aspects of girls' avoidance of interaction with boys. Less is known about why boys avoid interaction with girls, but the fact is that they do. In fact, their cross-sex avoidance appears to be even stronger. Thus, during middle childhood both boys and girls spend considerable portions of their social play time in groups of their own sex. This might not matter much for future relationships were it not for the fact that fairly distinctive styles of interaction develop in all-boy and all-girl groups. Thus, the segregated play groups constitute powerful socialization environments in which children acquire distinctive interaction skills that are adapted to same-sex partners. Sex-typed modes of interaction become consolidated, and I wish to argue that the distinctive patterns developed by the two sexes at this time have implications for the same-sex and cross-sex relationships that individuals form as they enter adolescence and adulthood.

It behooves us, then, to examine in somewhat more detail the nature of the interactive milieus that prevail in all-boy and all-girl groups. Elsewhere I have reviewed some of the findings of studies in which these two kinds of groups have been observed (Maccoby, 1988). Here I briefly summarize what we know.

The two sexes engage in fairly different kinds of activities and games (Huston, 1985). Boys play in somewhat larger groups, on the average, and their play is rougher (Humphreys & Smith, 1987) and takes up more space. Boys more often play in the streets and other public places; girls more often congregate in private homes or yards. Girls tend to form close, intimate friendships with one or two other girls, and these friendships are marked by the sharing of confidences (Kraft & Vraa, 1975). Boys' friendships, on the other hand, are more oriented around mutual interests in activities (Erwin, 1985). The breakup of girls' friendships is usually attended by more intense emotional reactions than is the case for boys.

For our present purposes, the most interesting thing about all-boy and all-girl groups is the divergence in the interactive styles that develop in them. In male groups, there is more concern with issues of dominance. Several psycholinguists have recorded the verbal exchanges that occur in these groups, and Maltz and Borker (1983) summarized the findings of several studies as follows: Boys in their groups are more likely than girls in all-girl groups to interrupt one another; use commands, threats, or boasts of authority; refuse to comply with another child's demand; give information; heckle a speaker; tell jokes or suspenseful stories; top someone else's story; or call another child names. Girls in all-groups, on the other hand, are more likely than boys to express agreement with what another speaker has just said, pause to give another girl a chance to speak, or when starting a speaking turn, acknowledge a point previously made by another speaker. This account indicates that among boys, speech serves largely egoistic functions and is used to establish and protect an individual's turf. Among girls, conversation is a more socially binding process.

In the past five years, analysts of discourse have done additional work on the kinds of interactive processes that are seen among girls, as compared with those among boys. The summary offered by Maltz and Borker has been both supported and extended. Sachs (1987) reported that girls soften their directives to partners, apparently attempting to keep them involved in a process of planning a play sequence, while boys are more likely simply to tell their partners what to do. Leaper (1989) observed children aged five and seven and found that verbal exchanges among girls more often take the form of what he called "collaborative speech acts" that involve positive reciprocity, whereas among boys, speech acts are more controlling and include more negative reciprocity. Miller and colleagues (Miller, Danaher, & Forbes, 1986) found that there was more conflict in boys' groups, and given that conflict had occurred, girls were more likely to use "conflict mitigating strategies," whereas boys more often used threats and physical force. Sheldon (1989) reported that when girls talk, they seem to have a double agenda: to be "nice" and sustain social relationships, while at the same time working to achieve their own individual ends. For boys, the agenda is more often the single one of self-assertion. Sheldon (1989) has noted that in interactions among themselves, girls are *not* unassertive. Rather, girls do successfully pursue their own ends, but they do so while toning down coercion and dominance, trying to bring about agreement, and restoring or maintaining group functioning. It should be noted that boys' confrontational style does not necessarily impede effective group functioning, as evidenced by boys' ability to cooperate with teammates for sports. A second point is that although researchers' own gender has been found to influence to some degree the kinds of questions posed and the answers obtained, the summary provided here includes the work of both male and female researchers, and their findings are consistent with one another.

As children move into adolescence and adulthood, what happens to the interactive styles that they developed in their largely segregated childhood groups? A first point to note is that despite the powerful attraction to members of the opposite sex in adolescence, gender segregation by no means disappears. Young people continue to spend a good portion of their social time with same-sex partners. In adulthood, there is extensive gender segregation in workplaces (Reskin, 1984), and in some societies and some social-class or ethnic groups, leisure time also is largely spent with same-sex others even after marriage. The literature on the nature of the interactions that occur among same-sex partners in adolescence and adulthood is quite extensive and cannot be reviewed here. Suffice it to say in summary that there is now considerable evidence that the interactive patterns found in sex-homogeneous dyads or groups in adolescence and adulthood are very similar to those that prevailed in the gender-segregated groups of childhood (e.g., Aries, 1976; Carli, 1989; Cowan, Drinkard, & MacGavin, 1984; Savin-Williams, 1979).

How can we summarize what it is that boys and girls, or men and women, are doing in their respective groups that distinguishes these groups from one another? There have been a number of efforts to find the major dimensions that best describe variations in interactive styles. Falbo and Peplau (1980) have factor analyzed a battery of measures and have identified two dimensions: one called direct versus indirect, the other unilateral versus bilateral. Hauser et al. (1987) have distinguished what they called *enabling* interactive styles from *constricting* or *restrictive* ones, and I believe this distinction fits the styles of the two sexes especially well. A restrictive style is one that tends to derail the interaction—to inhibit the partner or cause the partner to withdraw, thus shortening the interaction or bringing it to an end. Examples are threatening a partner, directly contradicting or interrupting, topping the partner's story, boasting, or engaging in other forms of self-display. Enabling or facilitative styles are those, such as acknowledging another's comment or expressing agreement, that support whatever the partner is doing and tend to keep the interaction going. I want to suggest that it is because women and girls use more enabling styles that they are able to form more intimate and more integrated relationships. Also I think it likely that it is the male concern for turf and dominance—that is, with not showing weakness to other men and boys—that underlies their restrictive interaction style and their lack of self-disclosure.

Carli (1989) has recently found that in discussions between pairs of adults, individuals are more easily influenced by a partner if that partner has just expressed agreement with them. In this work, women were quite successful in influencing one another in same-sex dyads, whereas pairs of men were less so. The sex difference was fully accounted for by the fact that men's male partners did not express agreement as often. Eagly (1987) has summarized data from a large number of studies on women's and men's susceptibility to influence and has found women to be somewhat more susceptible. Carli's work suggest that this tendency may not be a general female personality trait of "suggestibility" but may reflect the fact that women more often interact with other women who tend to express reciprocal agreement. Carli's finding resonates with some work with young children interacting with their mothers. Mary Parpal and I (Parpal & Maccoby, 1985) found that children were more compliant to a mother's demands if the two had previously engaged in a game in which the child was allowed to give directions that the mother followed. In other words, maternal compliance set up a system of reciprocity in which the child also complied. I submit that the same principle applies in adult interactions and that among women, influence is achieved in part by being open to influence from the partner.

Boys and men, on the other hand, although less successful in influencing one another in dyads, develop group structures—well-defined roles in games, dominance hierarchies, and team spirit—that appear to enable them to function effectively in groups. One may suppose that the male directive interactive style is less likely to derail interaction if and when group structural forces are in place. In other words, men and boys may *need* group structure more than women and girls do.

However, this hypothesis has yet to be tested in research. In any case, boys and men in their groups have more opportunity to learn how to function within hierarchical structures than do women and girls in theirs.

We have seen that throughout much of childhood and into adolescence and adulthood as well, people spend a good deal of their social time interacting with others of their own gender, and they continue to use distinctive interaction styles in these settings. What happens, then, when individuals from these two distinctive "cultures" attempt to interact with one another? People of both sexes are faced with a relatively unfamiliar situation to which they must adapt. Young women are less likely to receive the reciprocal agreement, opportunities to talk, and so on that they have learned to expect when interacting with female partners. Men have been accustomed to counter-dominance and competitive reactions to their own power assertions, and they now find themselves with partners who agree with them and otherwise offer enabling responses. It seems evident that this new partnership should be easier to adapt to for men than for women. There is evidence that men fall in love faster and report feeling more in love than do women early in intimate relationships (Huston & Ashmore, 1986). Furthermore, the higher rates of depression in females have their onset in adolescence, when rates of cross-sex interaction rise (Nolen-Hoeksema, in press). Although these phenomena are no doubt multidetermined, the asymmetries in interaction styles may contribute to them.

To some degree, men appear to bring to bear much the same kind of techniques in mixed-sex groups that they are accustomed to using in same-sex groups. If the group is attempting some sort of joint problem solving or is carrying out a joint task, men do more initiating, directing, and interrupting than do women. Men's voices are louder and are more listened to than women's voices by both sexes (West & Zimmerman, 1985); men are more likely than women to lose interest in a taped message if it is spoken in a woman's rather than a man's voice (Robinson & MacArthur, 1982). Men are less influenced by the opinions of other group members than are women. Perhaps as a consequence of their greater assertiveness, men have more influence on the group process (Lockheed, 1985; Pugh & Wahrman, 1983), just as they did in childhood. Eagly and colleagues (Eagly, Wood, & Fishbaugh, 1981) have drawn our attention to an important point about cross-sex interaction in groups: The greater resistance of men to being influenced by other group members is found only when the men are under surveillance, that is, if others know whether they have yielded to their partners' influence attempts. I suggest that it is especially the monitoring by other *men* that inhibits men from entering into reciprocal influence with partners. When other men are present, men appear to feel that they must guard their dominance status and not comply too readily lest it be interpreted as weakness.

Women's behavior in mixed groups is more complex. There is some work indicating that they adapt by becoming more like men—that they raise their voices, interrupt, and otherwise become more assertive than they would be when interacting with women (Carli, 1989; Hall & Braunwald, 1981). On the other hand, there is also evidence that they carryover some of their well-practiced female-style behaviors, sometimes in exaggerated form. Women may wait for a turn to speak that does not come, and thus they may end up talking less than they would in a women's group. They smile more than the men do, agree more often with what others have said, and give nonverbal signals of attentiveness to what others—perhaps especially the men—are saying (Duncan & Fiske, 1977). In some writings this female behavior has been referred to as "silent applause."

Eagly (1987) reported a meta-analysis of behavior of the two sexes in groups (mainly mixed-sex groups) that were performing joint tasks. She found a consistent tendency for men to engage in more task behavior-giving and receiving information, suggestions, and opinions (see also Aries, 1982)—whereas women are more likely to engage in socioemotional behaviors that support positive affective relations within the group. Which style contributes more to effective group process? It depends. Wood, Polek, and Aiken (1985) have compared the performance of all-female and all-male groups on different kinds of tasks, finding that groups of women have more success on tasks that require discussion and negotiation, whereas male groups do better on tasks where success depends on the volume of ideas being generated. Overall, it appears that *both* styles are productive, though in different ways.

There is evidence that women feel at a disadvantage in mixed-sex interaction. For example, Hogg and Turner (1987) set up a debate between two young men taking one position and two young women taking another. The outcomes in this situation were contrasted with a situation in which young men and women were debating against same-sex partners. After the cross-sex debate, the self-esteem of the young men rose, but that of the young women declined. Furthermore, the men liked their women opponents better after debating with them, whereas the women liked the men less. In other words, the encounter in most cases was a pleasurable experience for the men, but not for the women. Another example comes from the work of Davis (1978), who set up get-acquainted sessions between pairs of young men and women. He found that the men took control of the interaction, dictating the pace at which intimacy increased, whereas the women adapted themselves to the pace set by the men. The women reported later, however, that they had been uncomfortable about not being able to control the sequence of events, and they did not enjoy the encounter as much as the men did.

In adolescence and early adulthood, the powerful forces of sexual attraction come into play. When couples are beginning to fall in love, or even when they are merely entertaining the possibility of developing an intimate relationship, each is motivated to please the other, and each sends signals implying "Your wish is my command." There is evidence that whichever member of a couple is more attractive, or less in love, is at an advantage and is more able to influence the partner than vice versa (Peplau, 1979). The influence patterns based on the power of interpersonal attraction are not distinct in terms of gender; that is, it may be either the man or the woman in a courting relationship who has the influence advantage. When first meeting, or in the early stages of the acquaintance process, women still may feel at some disadvantage, as shown in the Davis study, but this situation need not last. Work done in the 1960s indicated that in many couples, as relationships become deeper and more enduring, any overall asymmetry in influence diminishes greatly (Heiss, 1962; Leik, 1963; Shaw & Sadler, 1965). Most couples develop a relationship that is based on communality rather than exchange bargaining. That is, they have many shared goals and work jointly to achieve them. They do not need to argue over turf because they have the same turf. In well-functioning married couples, both members of the pair strive to avoid conflict, and indeed there is evidence that the men on average are even more conflict-avoidant than the women (Gottman & Levenson, 1988; Kelley et al., 1978). Nevertheless, there are still carry-overs of the different interactive styles males and females have acquired at earlier points in the life cycle. Women seem to expend greater effort toward maintaining harmonious moods (Huston & Ashmore, 1986, p. 177). With intimate cross-sex partners, men use more direct styles of influence, and women use more indirect ones. Furthermore, women are more likely to withdraw (become silent, cold, and distant) and/or take unilateral action in order to get their way in a dispute (Falbo & Peplau, 1980), strategies that we suspect may reflect their greater difficulty in influencing a male partner through direct negotiation.

Space limitations do not allow considering in any depth the next set of important relationships that human beings form: that between parents and children. Let me simply say that I think there is evidence for the following: The interaction styles that women have developed in interaction with girls and other women serve them well when they become mothers. Especially when children are young, women enter into deeper levels of reciprocity with their children than do men (e.g., Gleason, 1987; Maccoby & Jacklin, 1983) and communicate with them better. On the other hand, especially after the first two years, children need firm direction as well as warmth and reciprocity, and fathers' styles may contribute especially well to this aspect of parenting. The relationship women develop with young children seems to depend very little on whether they are dealing with a son or a daughter; it builds on maternal response to the characteristics and needs of early childhood that are found in both boys and girls to similar degrees. Fathers, having a less intimate relationship with individual children, treat young boys and girls in a somewhat more gendered way (Siegal, 1987). As children approach middle childhood and interact with same-sex other children, they develop the interactive styles characteristic of their sex, and their parents more and more interact with them as they have always done with same-sex or opposite-sex others. That is, mothers and daughters develop greater intimacy and reciprocity: fathers and sons exhibit more friendly rivalry and joking, more joint interest in masculine activities, and more rough play. Nevertheless, there are many aspects of the relationships between parents and children that do not depend on the gender of either the parent or the child.

Obviously, as the scene unfolds across generations, it is very difficult to identify the point in the developmental cycle at which the interactional styles of the two sexes begin to diverge, and more important, to identify the forces that cause them to diverge. In my view, processes within the nuclear family have been given too much credit—or too much blame—for this aspect of sex-typing. I doubt that the development of distinctive interactive styles has much to do with the fact that children are parented primarily by women, as some have claimed (Chodorow, 1978; Gilligan, 1982), and it seems likely to me that children's "identification" with the same-sex parent is more a consequence than a cause of children's acquisition of sex-typed interaction styles. I would place most of the emphasis on the peer group as the setting in which children first discover the compatibility of same-sex others, in which boys first discover the requirements of maintaining one's status in the male hierarchy, and in which the gender of one's partners becomes supremely important. We do not have a clear answer to the ultimate question of why the segregated peer groups function as they do. We need now to think about how it can be answered. The answer is important if we are to adapt ourselves successfully to the rapid changes in the roles and relationships of the two sexes that are occurring in modern societies.

REFERENCES

Aries, E. (1976). Interaction patterns and themes of male, female, and mixed groups. *Small Group Behavior, 7,* 7–18.

Aries, E. J. (1982). Verbal and nonverbal behavior in single-sex and mixed-sex groups: Are traditional sex roles changing? *Psychological Reports, 51,* 127–134.

Block, J. H. (1976). Debatable conclusions about sex differences. *Contemporary Psychology, 21,* 517–522.

Carli, L. L. (1989). Gender differences in interaction style and influence. *Journal of Personality and Social Psychology, 56,* 565–576.

Chodorow, N. (1978). *The reproduction of mothering.* Berkeley, CA: University of California Press.

Cowan, C., Drinkard, J., & MacGavin. L. (1984). The effects of target, age and gender on use of power strategies.

Journal of Personality and Social Psychology, 47, 1391–1398.

Davis, J. D. (1978). When boy meets girl: Sex roles and the negotiation of intimacy in an acquaintance exercise. *Journal of Personality and Social Psychology, 36,* 684–692.

Duncan. S., Jr., & Fiske. D. W. (1977). *Face-to-face interaction: Research methods and theory.* Hillsdale, NJ: Erlbaum.

Eagly, A. H. (1983). Gender and social influence. *American Psychologist, 38,* 971–981.

Eagly, A. H. (1987). *Sex differences in social behavior: A social role interpretation.* Hillsdale, NJ: Erlbaum.

Eagly, A. H., Wood, W., & Fishbaugh. L. (1981). Sex differences in conformity: Surveillance by the group as a determinant of male non-conformity. *Journal of Personality and Social Psychology, 40,* 384–394.

Eisenhart, M. A., & Holland, D. C. (1983). Learning gender from peers: The role of peer group in the cultural transmission of gender. *Human Organization, 42,* 321–332.

Erwin. P. (1985). Similarity of attitudes and constructs in children's friendships. *Journal of Experimental Child Psychology, 40,* 470–485.

Fagot, B. I. (1985). Beyond the reinforcement principle: Another step toward understanding sex roles. *Developmental Psychology, 21,* 1097–1104.

Falbo, T,. & Peplau. L. A. (1980). Power strategies in intimate relationships. *Journal of Personality and Social Psychology, 38,* 618–628.

Gilligan, C. (1982). *In a different voice: Psychological theory and women's development.* Cambridge. MA: Howard University Press.

Gleason, J. B. (1987). Sex differences in parent-child interaction. In S. U. Phillips, S. Steele, & C. Tanz (Eds.), *Language, gender and sex in comparative perspective* (pp. 189–199). Cambridge, England: Cambridge University Press.

Gottman, J. M., & Levenson, R. W. (1988). The social psychophysiology of marriage. In P. Roller & M. A. Fitzpatrick (Eds.), *Perspectives on marital interaction* (pp. 182–200). New York: Taylor & Francis.

Greeno, C. G. (1989). *Gender differences in children's proximity to adults.* Unpublished doctoral dissertation. Stanford University, Stanford, CA.

Hall, J. A., & Braunwald, K. G. (1981). Gender cues in conversation. *Journal of Personality and Social Psychology, 40,* 99–110.

Hauser, S. T., Powers, S. I., Weiss-Perry, B., Follansbee, D. J., Rajapark, D., & Greene, W. M. (1987). *The constraining and enabling coding system manual.* Unpublished manuscript.

Heiss, J. S. (1962). Degree of intimacy and male-female interaction. *Sociometry, 25,* 197–208.

Hogg, M. A., & Turner. J. C. (1987). Intergroup behavior, self stereotyping and the salience of social categories. *British Journal of Social Psychology, 26,* 325–340.

Humphreys, A. P., & Smith, P. K. (1987). Rough and tumble friendship and dominance in school children: Evidence for continuity and change with age in middle childhood. *Child Development, 58,* 201–212.

Huston, A. C. (1985). The development of sex-typing: Themes from recent research. *Developmental Review, 5,* 1–17.

Huston, T. L., & Ashmore, R. D. (1986). Women and men in personal relationship. In R. D. Ashmore & R. K. Del Boca (Eds.), *The social psychology of female-male relations.* New York: Academic Press.

Jacklin, C. N., & Maccoby, E. E. (1978). Social behavior at 33 months in same-sex and mixed-sex dyads. *Child Development, 49,* 557–569.

Kelley, H. H., Cunningham, J. D., Grisham, J. A., Lefebvre, L. M., Sink, C. R., & Yablon, G. (1978). Sex differences in comments made during conflict in close relationships. *Sex Roles, 4,* 473–491.

Kraft, L. W., & Vraa. C. W. (1975). Sex composition of groups and pattern of self-disclosure by high school females. *Psychological Reports, 37,* 733–734.

Leaper, C. (1989). *The sequencing of power and involvement in boys' and girls' talk.* Unpublished manuscript (under review), University of California, Santa Cruz.

Leik, R. K. (1963). Instrumentality and emotionality in family interaction. *Sociometry, 26,* 131–145.

Lockheed, M. E. (1985). Sex and social influence: A meta-analysis guided by theory. In J. Berger & M. Zelditch (Eds.), *Status, attributions, and rewards* (pp. 406–429). San Francisco, CA: Jossey-Bass.

Maccoby, E. E. (1988). Gender as a social category. *Developmental Psychology, 26,* 755–765.

Maccoby, E. E., & Jacklin, C. N. (1974). *The psychology of sex differences.* Stanford, CA: Stanford University Press.

Maccoby, E. E., & Jacklin, C. N. (1980). Sex differences in aggression: A rejoinder and reprise. *Child Development, 51,* 964–980.

Maccoby, E. E., & Jacklin, C. N. (1983). The "person" characteristics of children and the family as environment. In D. Magnusson & V. L. Allen (Eds.), *Human development: An interactional perspective* (pp. 76–92). New York: Academic Press.

Maccoby, E. E., &. Jacklin, C. N. (1987). Gender segregation in childhood. In H. W. Reese (Ed.), *Advances in child development and behavior* (Vol. 20, pp. 239–288). New York: Academic Press.

Maltz, D. N., & Borker, R. A. (1983). A cultural approach to male-female miscommunication. In John A. Gumperz (Ed.), *Language and social identity* (pp. 195–216). New York: Cambridge University Press.

Miller, P., Danaher, D., & Forbes, D. (1986). Sex-related strategies for coping with interpersonal conflict in children aged five and seven. *Developmental Psychology, 22,* 543–548.

Nolen-Hoeksema, S. (in press). *Sex differences in depression.* Stanford, CA: Stanford University Press.

Parpal, M., & Maccoby, E. E. (1985). Maternal responsiveness and subsequent child compliance. *Child Development, 56,* 1326–1334.

Peplau, A. (1979). Power in dating relationships. In J. Freeman (Ed.), *Women: A feminist perspective* (pp. 121–137). Palo Alto, CA: Mayfield.

Powlishta, K. K. (1987, April). *The social context of cross-sex interactions.* Paper presented at biennial meeting of the Society for Research in Child Development, Baltimore, MD.

Powlishta, K. K. (1989). *Salience of group membership: The case of gender.* Unpublished doctoral dissertation. Stanford University, Stanford, CA.

Pruitt, D. G. (1976). Power and bargaining. In B. Seidenberg & A. Snadowsky (Eds.), *Social psychology: An introduction* (pp. 343–375). New York: Free Press.

Pugh, M. D., & Wahrman, R. (1983). Neutralizing sexism in mixed-sex groups: Do women have to be better than men? *American Journal of Sociology, 88,* 746–761.

Reskin, B. F. (Ed.). (1984). *Sex segregation in the workplace: Trends, explanations and remedies.* Washington, DC: National Academy Press.

Robinson, J., & McArthur, L. Z. (1982). Impact of salient vocal qualities on causal attribution for a speaker's behavior. *Journal of Personality and Social Psychology, 43,* 236–247.

Sachs, J. (1987). Preschool boys' and girls' language use in pretend play. In S. U. Phillips, S. Steele, & C. Tanz (Eds.), *Language, gender and sex in comparative perspective* (pp. 178–188). Cambridge, England: Cambridge University Press.

Savin-Williams, R. C. (1979). Dominance hierarchies in groups of early adolescents. *Child Development, 50,* 923–935.

Serbin, L. A., Sprafkin, C., Elman, M., & Doyle, A. (1984). The early development of sex differentiated patterns of social influence. *Canadian Journal of Social Science, 14,* 350–363.

Shaw, M. E., & Sadler, O. W. (1965). Interaction patterns in heterosexual dyads varying in degree of intimacy. *Journal of Social Psychology, 66,* 345–351.

Sheldon, A. (1989, April). *Conflict tal:. Sociolinguistic challenges to self-assertion and how young girls meet them.* Paper presented at the biennial meeting of the Society for Research in Child Development, Kansas City.

Siegal, M. (1987). Are sons and daughters treated more differently by fathers than mothers? *Developmental Review, 7,* 183–209.

Thorne, B. (1986). Girls and boys together, but mostly apart. In W. W. Hartup & L. Rubin (Eds.), *Relationships and development* (pp. 167–184). Hillsdale, NJ: Erlbaum.

Tieger, T. (1980). On the biological basis of sex differences in aggression. *Child Development, 51,* 943–963.

Wasserman, G. A., & Stern, D. N. (1978). An early manifestation of differential behavior toward children of the same and opposite sex. *Journal of Genetic Psychology, 133,* 129–137.

West, C., & Zimmerman. D. H. (1985). Gender, language and discourse. In T. A. van Dijk (Ed.), *Handbook of discourse analysis: Vol. 4, Discourse analysis in society* (pp. 103–124). London: Academic Press.

Wood, W., Polek, D., & Aiken, C. (1985). Sex differences in group task performance. *Journal of Personality and Social Psychology, 48,* 63–71.

PART 2
SUMMARY OF THE SEX DIFFERENCES REPORTED BY MACCOBY (1990)

Summarize the sex differences in social behaviors as reported by Maccoby (1990). Given that her account is a developmental one, it would be useful to list these differences as they appear successively over childhood, adolescence, and adult life.

PART 3
DISCUSSION QUESTIONS

1. What advantage, if any, do you see in Maccoby's focus on social situations to document behavioral differences between the sexes as opposed to the more traditional focus on individual characteristics such as personality traits, emotional, and cognitive functioning?

2. In the introduction to this module, four reasons were mentioned that led Maccoby and Jacklin to regard with caution the sex differences they had reported in their book. Do you think that any of these reasons for caution would also apply to the new set of sex differences now reported by Maccoby?

3. Throughout her article, Maccoby reviews a number of factors that have been examined in attempts to explain the origin of the sex differences

she reports. What are these factors? Is she satisfied with the explanations offered so far for the origin of these differences, and why? How satisfied are you by these same explanations?

4. In the last paragraph of her article, Maccoby states that young children begin segregating themselves into same-sex play groups at a very young age. Then she asks: (1) "Why does this segregation take place and why at such a young age?"; and (2) "How do the sex-specific cultures thus created contribute to the developmental emergence of sex differences in behavior?" How would you answer these two questions?

5. The most pervasive and reliable difference in the literature on sex differences is that males are more aggressive, physically and verbally, than females. Given the following general definition of aggression, "any action intended to cause harm to another individual," can you think of typically feminine forms of aggression? Assuming the existence of sex-specific forms of aggression, would it be possible, in your opinion, to show that females can be as aggressive as males?

6. If you are a woman, do you resonate to the portrayal of the feminine behaviors as depicted by Maccoby in the article you read? Answer this question from the perspective of your cognitive and academic performances, and how you, yourself, behave in these respects in social settings when males are present and not present. Do you think that the same sex differences in social behaviors are still observed in contemporary adolescent males and females?

SUGGESTED READINGS

Björkqvist, K. (1994). Sex differences in physical, verbal, and indirect aggression: A review of recent research. *Sex Roles, 30,* 177–188.

Crick, N. (1996). The role of overt aggression, relation aggression, and prosocial behavior in the prediction of children's future social adjustment. *Child Development, 67,* 2317–2327.

Tieger, T. (1980). On the biological basis of sex differences in aggression. *Child Development, 51,* 943–963.

MODULE 19

GENDER STEREOTYPES IN TEEN MAGAZINES

In this module, you will examine gender stereotypes as revealed in teen magazines. Gender stereotypes are *the beliefs that members of an entire culture hold about the attitudes and behaviors that are acceptable and appropriate for males and females.* Communicated through a variety of means, the prescription of appropriate behaviors for males and females starts early in life. Media images are a powerful way to dissect some of these cultural messages.

PART 1
EXAMINE GENDER STEREOTYPES IN TEEN MAGAZINES

Find a current issue of a teen magazine geared toward your own gender. If you can, also find a periodical geared toward an adolescent audience that includes images and messages that run contrary to typical gender stereotypes. Leaf through the pages and generate a list of gender stereotypes portrayed for both males and females. Note specific behaviors, images, and attitudes.

PART 2
DISCUSSION QUESTIONS

1. What do the advertisements and articles reveal about behaviors that are acceptable or appropriate for males and females? Give some specific examples. How do these contribute to gender-based beliefs and gender-typing? Are these messages obvious or subtle? Are there contradictory messages?

2. Are the stereotypes of females more rigid or more flexible than those of males? Do any of the images or articles suggest consequences to breaking gender-appropriate behavior? Give specific examples.

3. Look at the table of contents. What does this say important parts of life are for a male or female of this age?

4. In what ways does the language used in the magazine enforce or reinforce gendered behaviors and/or attitudes?

5. In your experience, how do you think the media affected your gendered behavior? What were some other ways you became aware of gender stereotypes?

6. Based on what you know of cognitive and social abilities, how might media images differentially or similarly affect gender beliefs for a 6 year old, a 12 year old, and a 16 year old?

■ SUGGESTED READINGS

Ruble, D. N., & Martin, C. L. (1998). Gender development. In N. Eisenberg (Vol. Ed.), *Social, emotional, and personality development*, Vol 3. (pp. 933–1016), of W. Damon (Gen. Ed.), *Handbook of child psychology.* New York: Wiley.

Eckes, Thomas & Trautner, Hanns M. (Eds). (2000). *The developmental social psychology of gender.* Mahwah, N.J.: Lawrence Erlbaum Associates, Inc.

Beal, C. R. (1994). *Boys and girls: the development of gender roles.* New York: McGraw-Hill.

MODULE 20

Moral Development

In this module you will learn more about Lawrence Kohlberg's theory of moral development. You will also read several vignettes dealing with moral dilemmas to facilitate discussion about gender and age differences in moral development.

Introduction

The importance of moral development is that it establishes a basis for what is right and wrong, thus providing incentives for appropriate behavior in social situations and encouraging pro-social behavior.

The development of moral reasoning is the process by which children assume their society's standards of right and wrong. Kohlberg believed that the development of moral reasoning was related to the development of cognitive ability, and that therefore, moral reasoning changes as a function of cognitive development. In Kohlberg's theory, moral development progresses through a universal and invariant sequence, with each stage building upon the previous stage. Kohlberg's theory divides moral development into three broad levels, with each level consisting of two separate stages.

LEVEL 1
Preconventional Morality

Rules are externally guided instead of being internalized.

Stage 1: Punishment and Obedience Orientation: The consequences of an action determine whether the act is considered good or bad.

Stage 2: Instrumental Hedonism: An individual conforms to rules so he or she can gain rewards and/or fulfill personal desires.

LEVEL 2
CONVENTIONAL MORALITY

The individual has internalized many moral values, and he or she wants to follow the rules that have been set by others such as mother, father, or teachers. This internalization drives the individual to want to please authority figures, as the beliefs and perspectives of authority figures are very important to him or her.

Stage 3: *"Good boy" or "good girl" morality:* Right and wrong are determined by the approval of others.

Stage 4: *Authority and social-order maintaining morality:* The individual now believes that it is right to conform to the society's rules and laws. The belief that these laws and rules maintain social order is the basis for the individual's conformity.

LEVEL 3
POSTCONVENTIONAL MORALITY

The individual defines what is right and wrong from a perspective on justice that may not correspond with the views of authority figures. While he or she takes into consideration society's rules and laws, he or she has differing views that guide moral decision-making. Whereas the individual previously only took the perspective of a particular authority figure or group, he or she now takes the perspective of all individuals.

Stage 5: *Morality of contract, individual rights, and democratically accepted law:* This stage is characterized by a deeper understanding of the underlying purpose that laws and rules serve. There is also a concern that laws are arrived at by a democratic process in order to ensure maximum social welfare.

Stage 6: *Morality of individual principles of conscience:* Right and wrong are based on self-chosen principles. The individual arrives at these principles through abstract thought and reasoning, while taking the perspective of all others. Kohlberg believed this stage to be the ideal in moral reasoning, but he rarely observed this stage.

One strategy for assessing a child's level of moral development is to present a moral dilemma and ask the child to respond to questions about that dilemma. Here is an example of the so-called *Heinz dilemma* used by Colby et al. 1983:

> In Europe, a woman was near death from a special kind of cancer. There was one drug that the doctors thought might save her. It was a form of radium that a druggist in the same town had recently discovered. The drug was expensive to make, but the druggist was charging 10 times what the drug cost him to make. He paid $200 for the radium and charged $2000 for a small dose of the drug. The sick woman's husband, Heinz, went to everyone he knew to borrow the money, but he could only get together about $1000, which is half of what it

cost. He told the druggist that his wife was dying and asked him to sell it cheaper or let him pay later. But the druggist said, "No, I discovered the drug and I'm going to make money from it." So Heinz gets desperate and considers breaking into the man's store to steal the drug for his wife.

PART 1
RESPONSES TO THE DILEMMA

Here are some typical responses to the Heinz dilemma from children at various levels of morality. On the basis of the levels described above, try to code the stage of morality for each child.

1. I feel bad that Heinz's wife might die, but she might live too. Heinz shouldn't steal the drug if he wants to do the right thing. People can't just do what they always want to do. My dad says we all have to live together, and that means we have to use self-control. I think Heinz should listen to my dad and not steal the drug. What if everybody just started stealing and doing bad stuff? Well then, everything would just be crazy. Nobody would be safe and all kind of bad stuff would be happening to everybody. Heinz could start something that would be bad for everybody, including him and his wife.

Level: _____
Stage: _____

2. Well, I don't think Heinz should steal the drug because stealing is wrong, Heinz will get in a lot of trouble if he steals the drug. I wouldn't want to get in trouble for something like that. What if Heinz goes to jail? Then his wife would be mad at him for getting in trouble. Maybe Heinz's wife will get better and she won't need the drug after all. I just don't think it's a good idea to steal because if you get caught you'll get in trouble.

Level: _____
Stage: _____

3. The druggist is doing the wrong thing by not giving Heinz the drug. If we really believe in the philosophy that human life is valuable, then we wouldn't want someone to die just because they didn't have the money to pay for drugs or services. I mean seriously, that's going against the golden rule and everything. If the druggist were in Heinz's position, he would want somebody to do the right thing and save his loved one. The druggist's decision to not share the medicine with Heinz is not morally right, even if it is legal. This is a case where it would be good for Heinz to break the law because he would be doing a greater good by saving his wife.

Level: _____
Stage: _____

4. Well, I think you should consider the feelings of everybody involved. How will Heinz's decision to steal the drug affect him, his wife, and the druggist? If Heinz steals the drug and then the druggist goes broke and he ends up losing his business, I don't think Heinz should steal the drug. However, if the druggist has enough money to do without the $1000, then Heinz should steal the drug because his wife's life is worth more than any dollar amount. I don't think Heinz's wife should die. I wish Heinz could get the drug, but not if it's going to make the druggist go out of business and then druggist's family might die too. Maybe Heinz can apply for a loan and the druggist will get his money and Heinz's wife will live. That way, everybody will get what they need.

Level: _____
Stage: _____

5. He shouldn't steal the drug because he will be arrested by the police and put in jail. Stealing is wrong. My mom told me that if I steal, I would have to pay it back. Plus, people would think I was a bad person. People will think Heinz is a bad person if he steals because everybody knows that stealing is against the law. If people think Heinz is a bad person, they won't be nice to him and he won't have friends. Heinz should do the right thing and follow the rules so things will work out good for him, instead of

trying to do things his own way and getting himself into trouble.

Level: _____
Stage: _____

6. Heinz should definitely steal the drug. It's ridiculous that the druggist won't give him the drug. That's just not fair of the druggist because Heinz is poor, and he was willing to pay all he could and pay the rest later. The druggist could probably afford to put Heinz on a payment plan. It's the druggist's responsibility to give people medicine. That's his job. If he's not going to give people medicine—well, he should just retire.

Level: _____
Stage: _____

PART 2
■ DISCUSSION QUESTIONS

1. What other techniques might be used to assess an individual's level of moral reasoning?
2. What factors do you think might affect the rate at which a person passes through the stages of moral development? Consider both internal and external influences.
3. Recent research using Kohlbeg's theory reports that people who live in non-Western societies do not reach the post-conventional level of moral reasoning. What does this say about the mechanisms whereby we acquire our moral standards? What does this say about the generality of Kohlberg's theory?
4. Do you think it is possible for an individual to be at a certain stage of moral reasoning, but his or her actions not reflect this level of moral reasoning? Why would this happen? What factors might cause someone to act in contradiction of his or her internalized moral values?

■ SUGGESTED READINGS

Colby, A., Kohlberg, L., Gibbs, J., & Lieberman, M. (1983). A longitudinal study of moral judgment. *Monographs of the Society for Research in Child Development, 48,* (1–2, Serial No. 200).

Kohlberg, L. (1984). *The psychology of moral development: the nature and validity of moral stages.* San Francisco, CA: Harper & Row.

Kohlberg, L. (1987). *Child psychology and childhood education: a cognitive/developmental view.* New York, NY: Longman.

Answers:
1. James, age 12 (Conventional Morality—Stage 3)
2. Sarah, age 8 (Preconventional Morality—Stage 1)
3. Kelly, age 16 (Postconventional Morality—Stage 5)
4. Herbert, age 16 (Postconventional Morality—Stage 6)
5. Mike, age 8 (Preconventional Morality—Stage 2)
6. Janet, age 12 (Conventional Morality—Stage 4)

Langford, P. E. (1995). *Approaches to the development of moral reasoning.* Hove, UK: Lawrence Erlbaum Associates.

Laupa, M. (2000). *Rights and wrongs: how children and young adults evaluate the world.* San Francisco, CA: Jossey-Bass.

Rest, J. R. (1999). *Postconventional moral thinking: a Neo-Kohlbergian approach.* Mahwah, N.J.: Lawrence Erlbaum Associates.

Saltzstein, H. D. (1997). *Culture as a context for moral development: new perspectives on the particular and the universal.* San Francisco, CA: Jossey-Bass.

Sigelman, C. K. & Shaffer, D. R. (1995). *Life-span human development.* Belmont, CA: Wadsworth Inc.

MODULE 21

TELEVISION VIOLENCE AND AGGRESSION

There is considerable debate over whether or not television is too violent. This module will provide you with information regarding children's television viewing and violence levels in television programming. You will also be asked to view a show intended for children and take notes regarding aggressive acts displayed in the show. Questions are posed to facilitate a discussion of this topic.

■ INTRODUCTION

A number of arguments have been offered concerning the negative effects of televised violence on children. From a behavioral perspective, repeated exposure to such stimulation could serve to desensitize children to the types of cruel and aggressive acts being shown. Consequently, over time, they would react less strongly to such depictions and possibly to real-life violence. From a social learning perspective, behavior portrayed on the screen becomes a model for children to imitate. In other words, the more violence and aggression children watch, the more violent and aggressive they are likely to act themselves.

Counter arguments often focus on the idea that *reality is harsh*. This point of view maintains that television merely reflects the violence present in society and that children are exposed to such images anyway.

A great deal of research has been compiled on the violence in television and its impact on children. Part 1 of this module points you to a series of reports from the UCLA Center for Communication Policy documenting violence on television. Part 2 of the module is an assignment for you to do some television viewing and data collection of your own. Finally, Part 3 of the module provides thought questions about this topic.

PART 1
■ CURRENT STATISTICS ON TELEVISION VIOLENCE

Visit http://ccp.ucla.edu/pages/VReports.asp to obtain statistics on current estimates of the level of violent programming on television.

PART 2
MAKE YOUR OWN ESTIMATION OF TELEVISION VIOLENCE

Watch a television program that children might watch. Most children's viewing occurs on weekdays in the late afternoon or early evening or on Saturdays in the morning. Record the title, date, and time of the program. Take note of the aggressive acts displayed in the show. You may want to develop a brief data sheet to keep track of your observations. For example, you may want to note different types of violence and aggression (e.g., fantasy versus real, physical versus verbal, etc.).

PART 3
DISCUSSION QUESTIONS

1. What evidence would you present to defend the argument that television is too violent? Conversely, what evidence would you present to argue it is not?
2. What messages do you think children are receiving from their television viewing about attitudes toward violence and aggression in this culture?
3. Do you think that television has an impact on children's aggressive behavior? Conversely, do you think it affects their prosocial behavior?
4. Think about your own television viewing habits when you were a child. What did you learn from television? Did anything you watched scare you? Did anything you watched confuse you? To what extent do you think your childhood viewing habits shaped your current viewing habits?
5. Imagine you are the parent of children of different ages: preschool, middle childhood, adolescence. How would you guide each of your children's television viewing? What "rules" would you have? Would they differ by age? Would you monitor the amount and type of shows they watch? How? Would you watch with them? Why or why not?
6. What responsibilities do you feel are held by the television industry or the government to monitor the amount and content of children's television programming?

SUGGESTED READINGS

http://www.apa.org/pubinfo/violence.html

Huston, A. C., Wright, J. C. (1998). Mass media and children's development. In W. Damon (Gen. Ed.), I. E. Segal, & K. A. Renninger (Vol. Eds.), *Handbook of child psychology: Vol. 4. Child psychology in practice* (pp. 999–1058). New York: Wiley.

MODULE 22

SELECTIVE BREEDING FOR HIGH AND LOW AGGRESSION

Is there a gene for aggression? A gene that predisposes people to addiction? The belief that there is a one-to-one correspondence between specific genes and specific behaviors is widespread in the public. In this module we ask you to take a second look at this notion by examining the behavioral and developmental effects of selective breeding for high and low aggression in mice. In the first part, two graphs are presented showing how social reactivity and social inhibition (or freezing) develop in mouse lines selectively bred for high and low aggression. Then, the discussion section asks what these graphs suggest concerning the relations between genes and behavior.

INTRODUCTION

Some 30 years ago, Robert B. Cairns at UNC-Chapel Hill used selective breeding to produce mouse lines that differ markedly in their aggressive tendencies (see Cairns, McCombie, & Hood, 1983). To produce these lines, he began by purchasing a "foundational stock" of pregnant female mice that delivered babies a few days later. When the babies reached 21 days of age, he removed them from their mother, isolated all the males in single cages and placed their sisters together in other cages, keeping track of who their brothers were. Social isolation was used because it is known to induce aggressive behavior in male mice. It also guarantees that the subjects will have had no fighting experience by the time their *innate* tendency to attack other males is evaluated. When these isolated males reached young adulthood (42 days) he determined how aggressive they were. To do this he had every male interact for 10 minutes with another male in a small compartment, and he counted the number of attacks they initiated. The partner males they interacted with were of the same age and weight. The only thing that distinguished them from the subjects was that up to the time they were used as partners, they had been reared in groups of four other males instead of being isolated. The rationale for this difference in rearing history was that group conditions have an inhibiting effect on mice aggressive tendencies, so that when attacks occurred in dyadic tests, they were very likely to be initiated by the isolated males and not by their partners. In this way, Cairns was able to obtain relatively pure measures of how aggressive his isolated males were. All subjects were tested only once and a fresh partner male was used in every test so that there was no carry-over effects of prior exposure to fighting in the test condition.

With a total of 100 males observed in these dyadic tests, Cairns obtained a nice normal curve with a mean number of attacks of about 10 and a bunch of animals at both extremes of the distribution that either attacked a lot, or very rarely. On this basis, he identified the 25 males that had the highest attack scores and the 25 that had the lowest scores, and he mated them to sisters of other males that met the same criterion. The remaining 50 males with attack scores closer to the mean were not mated and their genes were thus removed from the gene pool. The progeny of these parents was again tested in dyadic encounters under the same conditions. This time, Cairns removed from the gene pool the sons of high-aggressive fathers that had the lowest attack scores in dyadic testing, and, in the other group, he removed the sons of the low-aggressive fathers that had the highest attack scores. It took only four generations of repeating this process before a large and statistically reliable difference was obtained between the two mouse sub-populations. He called the high-aggressive line NC900 and the low-aggressive line NC100. (NC means North Carolina.)

This selective breeding program was passed on after 13 generations to a colleague (Gariepy, at UNC-CH) who continued to use the same selective breeding criteria to perpetuate the NC900 and NC100 mouse lines. Now in its 40th generation, these selected lines have continued from the 4th generation onward to produce high-aggressive males that predictably attack with high frequencies in 10-minute dyadic tests following isolation (i.e., 25–45 attacks on average) and low-aggressive males that attack very rarely (i.e., 0 to 3 attacks on average) when tested for the first time in young adulthood.

Perhaps, the selective breeding program best known to students is the one initiated by Tryon in 1929 that proceeded the famous bright and dull rat lines. You remember that the bright rats learned to run a maze without making errors in a few trials only, while the dull rats took many more trials to achieve the same performance. When Tryon published his results he presented them as evidence that intelligence was genetically determined. The NC selective breeding program could be similarly held as evidence that there is a genetic basis for aggression. As you are about to see, such a conclusion may be an oversimplification of what is really going on. In the first part of this module you will study two graphs, one that depicts for each selected line the development of social reactivity, and the other, the development of social inhibition (also called freezing). On this basis, we ask what these developmental trends suggest concerning the relation between genetic background and aggressive behavior.

PART 1
Correlated Effects of Selective Breeding

As a rule, investigators who have used selective breeding to produce mouse or rat lines that differ on a specific behavioral trait find that the differences between their selected lines far exceed the single criterion behavior they targeted for selection. The NC100 and NC900 mouse lines are no exception. In this particular case, selection for differential aggression also produced large differences in temperament and its underlying neurochemistry. The high-aggressive animals are very reactive and show little inhibition in social encounters while the low-aggressive ones are very timid, inhibited, and show little reactivity. Consistent with these differences, neurochemical analyses have shown that NC900 have higher concentrations of dopamine in the nucleus accumbens and caudate nucleus than the low-aggressive animals. The latter, in turn, have higher concentrations of serotonin in the amygdala and a higher concentration of GABA receptors in prefrontal cortex (see Gariepy et al. 1996; full reference provided below). Line differences were also found in maze learning, maternal behaviors, open-field activity, behavioral and physiological responses to stress, and in responses to a number of pharmacological agents. Here we focus on correlated effects of selective breeding on social reactivity and social inhibition.

Next to the propensity to attack in a dyadic test, a most conspicuous difference between the two lines is that the NC100 males, when approached by the partner animal, tend to freeze. That is, they become immobile, adopt a rigid freezing posture, and do not respond much to social stimulation (i.e., they appear inhibited). This is observed even when the partner approaches in a non-threatening fashion and only mildly contacts the subject. This tendency became evident in the 4th generation and continued to increase over 15 generations, even if the maximum line difference in attack behaviors was reached by the 8th generation. The high-aggressive males, by contrast, rarely freeze in dyadic encounters and attack fiercely instead. It has been determined in behavioral analyses that freezing reduces both the probability that social interactions will escalate to attacks (Gariepy et al., 1988) and the tendency of the partner males to engage low-aggressive subjects in further social interactions (Bauer & Gariepy, 2001).

Social reactivity is another behavioral domain that strongly differentiates the males of the NC100 and NC900 lines. Prior to attacking, high-aggressive males often tend to respond very reactively to the mild investigative approaches made to them by the partner animal. This reactivity takes the following form: When approached in a non-threatening fashion, NC900 subjects often exhibit a startling response and adopt a boxing posture accompanied by high-pitched vocalizations. In the most extreme cases they rapidly jump away and escape from the partner subject. This behavior is much less frequent in the low-aggressive line and when it occurs it is rarely expressed in the more extreme form of sudden jumps. It has been shown in functional analyses that this reactivity has two important consequences. First, it causes the partner animal to show defensive behaviors, to become reactive in turn, and in some cases, to attack proactively. Second, the more reactive NC900 males are often those that attack the most rapidly and the most frequently in dyadic tests.

The Development of the Freezing Response as a Function of Line

The development of the propensity to freeze upon social contact was examined in NC100 and NC900 males from 21 to 45 days of age. The developmental function of this behavior was of interest to the investigators because freezing is a natural response among young rodents when, shortly after weaning, they begin exploring the environment on their own. This response rapidly disappears as the animals become more familiar with their environment and better equipped to defend themselves. Given that the capacity to launch full fledged attacks is not established before 30 to 32 days of age in mice, the goal was to determine what the developmental time course of this behavior would look like among high- and low-aggressive males and whether its rate of extinction over development would differ between the two lines.

Freeze frequency during a 10-minute dyadic test.

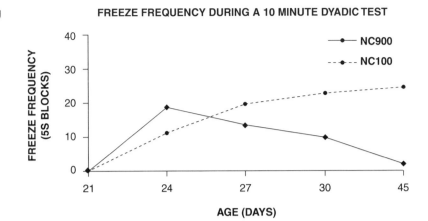

Reactive behavior during a 10-minute dyadic test.

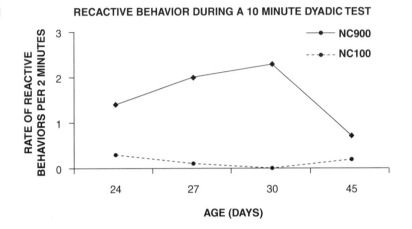

The animals used to generate this figure were tested only once in a dyadic test, either at 21, 24, 27, 30, or 45 days of age. Those tested at day 21 were taken directly from their mother, prior to any isolation experience. The other animals were isolated at weaning (day 21) and they were tested either after 3 days in isolation (day 24), 6 days (day 27), 9 days (day 30), or 24 days (day 45). Note that freezing is not observed at 21 days of age when the subjects are simply removed from their litter and exposed to another male in a dyadic encounter.

The Development of Social Reactivity as a Function of Line

Social reactivity was defined as the sum of the following behaviors: Startle, kicking (rapid reflexive-like extension of the posterior leg), high-pitched vocalization, boxing posture, jumping, and escaping. To be counted as reactive responses, these behaviors had to occur only in response to non-threatening, mild stimulation from the partner, and prior to the occurrence of any agonistic behavior in the dyadic test. These criteria were used because following attacks animals often display reactive behaviors. Because the window of time for observing reactivity was not the same for all subjects data are presented as rates per 2 minutes instead of frequencies.

Reactive responses were observed in the same subjects as those used to generate the previous figure under the same conditions. No reactive behaviors were observed at 21 days of age (data not presented).

PART 2
Discussion Questions

1. Attack frequency was the only criterion ever used in this selective breeding program to produce the NC100 and NC900 lines. How do you explain that these lines show differences in several behaviors and neurochemical functions that were never directly targeted for selection?

2. Given the information provided in the introduction to this module, explain why selective breeding for differential aggression also produced a large difference in social reactivity as shown in the second figure? As a hint, consider that selection for low-aggression may impose constraints on the expression of reactive behaviors.

3. Stephen J. Gould (1977) suggested that an efficient way to promote evolution is to produce descendants that retain longer in their development the juvenile characteristics of their ancestors (i.e., neoteny or *holding on to youth*). Given what you read in the introduction on the development of freezing in mice, speculate on the possibility that selecting for low aggression may favor a progressive neotenization of the freezing response? How would the developmental function of this behavior change across successive generations if freezing had undergone a progressive neotenization in the NC100 line?

4. Imagine that instead of testing high- and low-aggressive animals against a standard male partner we would arrange dyadic encounters between high and low-aggressive subjects. Do you think NC900 males would look as aggressive as they do with a standard partner and that low-aggressive animals would look as inhibited? Do you think low-aggressive animals would defend themselves if attacked? Provide a rationale for your answers.

5. At this point of your discussion, do you think that there is a gene for aggression? If you think so, explain how this is consistent with your answers to the previous questions. If you do not think so, explain how selective breeding may produce differences in aggression.

6. Is this research relevant to our understanding of individual difference in aggressive behavior in our species? Do you think the processes you referred to in your discussion of the previous questions would be of value to address this question, and why?

Suggested Readings

Bauer, D. J. & Gariepy, J.-L. (2001). The function of freezing in the social interactions of juvenile high- and low-aggressive mice. *Aggressive Behavior, 27*, 463–475.

Cairns, R. B., MacCombie, D. J., & Hood, K. E. (1983). A developmental-genetic analysis of aggressive behavior in mice: I. Behavioral outcomes. *Journal of Comparative Psychology, 97*, 69–89.

Gariepy, J.-L., Gendreau, P. J., Mailman, R. B., Tancer, M., & Lewis, M. H. (1995). Rearing conditions alter social reactivity and D_1 dopamine receptors in high and low aggressive mice. *Psychopharmacology, Biochemistry and Behavior, 51,* 767–773.

Gariepy, J.-L., Lewis, M. H., & Cairns, R. B. (1996). Genes, neurobiology, and aggression: Time frames and functions of social behaviors in adaptation. In D. M. Stoff and R. B. Cairns (Eds.), *Aggression and violence: Neurobiological, biosocial and genetic perspectives* (pp. 41–63). New York: Lawrence Erlbaum.

Gariepy, J.-L., Gendreau, P. L., Cairns, R. B., & Lewis, M. H. (1998). D_1 dopamine receptors and the reversal of isolation-induced behaviors in mice. *Behavioural Brain Research, 95,* 103–112.

Gariepy, J.-L., Bauer, D. J., & Cairns, R. B. (2001). Selective breeding for differential aggression in mice provides evidence for heterochrony in social behaviours. *Animal Behaviour, 61,* 933–947.

MODULE 23

JUVENILE DELINQUENCY

This module is designed to help you think about the development and stability of aggressive and criminal behavior in children and adolescents. It is also designed to facilitate thought and discussion about issues related to rehabilitation and prevention of these aggressive and criminal behaviors.

INTRODUCTION

Juvenile crime is a growing problem in our society. Violent offending usually begins in the adolescent years, and more than half of the persons who become involved in serious violent offenses prior to age 27 commit their first violent offense between the ages of 14 and 17. Almost all offenders commit their first act before age 21 (Elliot, 1994). Although most children occasionally display aggressive behaviors, prevalence studies have identified 5% to 10% of children as displaying clinically significant aggression or conduct problems (Offord, Boyle, & Racine, 1991).

Adolescent crime permeates all segments of society, including school, family, and community. Overall, violent crime in the United States has risen 600% since 1953 (Skogan, 1989), the majority of the rise occurring over the last twenty years. In 1999, law enforcement agencies made an estimated 2.5 million arrests of persons under the age of 18; of these, 1,400 were charged with murder or negligent manslaughter (Snyder & Sickmund, 1999). In the eyes of the American public, crime and violence now rank as one of the most important problems facing this country (Berke, 1994), with homicide the leading cause of death among urban males aged 15–24 (Huesmann & Miller, 1994).

Even more disturbing is that once children have become criminals it is difficult to change their developmental trajectory. As many as 60% to 84% of juvenile offenders will be re-arrested after their initial criminal offense (White, 2001). With such a high recidivism rate, there has long been a debate about the efficacy of rehabilitation for juvenile offenders. Some people would argue that rehabilitation programs are doomed to fail, while others insist that rehabilitation is our only hope of saving some of these lost children.

In Part 1 of this module, we have reprinted a newspaper article briefly discussing recidivism rates in juvenile delinquents (i.e., second incidents of the same criminal behavior), as well as researchers' suggestions regarding the role of education in recidivism rates. Part 2 poses questions in order to facilitate discussion of the topic.

PART 1
REQUIRED READING

JAILHOUSE EDUCATION CAN BREAK CYCLE OF CRIME

Earning a degree makes it less likely a released inmate will return

James White

From Charlotte Observer, *August 16, 2001 by James White. Copyright © 2001 by Charlotte Observer. Reprinted by permission.*

Teaching GED classes at the Mecklenburg County Jail this summer has been quite an experience. I teach three classes five days a week. The juveniles (16- to 17-year-olds) are in class 8:30–11:30 A.M. After lunch, the women come to class for 90 minutes, followed by two classes for the men in the afternoon and evening. The classes are mandatory for the juveniles and voluntary for the adults. I work with between 40 and 50 students daily. Not only is this the most demanding job I've ever had, but also the most rewarding.

At best this is a difficult environment for students to work in. Many of them face felony charges that carry stiff prison sentences. Others have substance abuse problems that need to be addressed before they can change the behavior that resulted in their incarceration. Some are there for the first time, but far too many have been there before and have not, as yet, broken the cycle of recidivism that plagues our criminal justice system. Through education, we're hoping that some of these students can and will make significant, positive changes in their lives.

Former U.S. Supreme Court Chief Justice Warren Burger said: "We must accept the reality that to confine offenders behind walls without trying to change them is an expensive folly with short-term benefits—winning battles while losing the war." In response to the public's growing fear of crime, many policymakers have promoted building more prisons and demanding harsher sentencing while eliminating various programs inside prisons and jails.

A report issued by the Congressional Subcommittee to Investigate Juvenile Delinquency estimates that the national recidivism rate for juvenile offenders is between 60 percent and 84 percent, while the re-arrest rate for adults is around 64 percent. Research shows that quality education is one of the most effective factors in decreasing the likelihood that people will return to crime after release.

A 1998 Federal Bureau of Prisons study found that obtaining a GED could decrease the likelihood of re-arrest of parolees by more than 20 percent and showed that the higher the education level, the lower the recidivism rate. Inmates with at least two years of college education have a re-arrest rate of only 10 percent, and for those who earned a four-year college degree, re-arrest was almost nonexistent. Fortunately, those who make decisions concerning inmate programs in the Charlotte area have chosen to accept the research findings and make education a high priority.

What does this all mean to us? In just the past two months eight men and women have earned their GEDs while in jail in Mecklenburg County. At that rate, nearly 50 inmates will take that first important step to obtaining their college degrees this year alone. It means that instead of 30 of them returning to a life of crime while 20 do not, the figures will be reversed. There will be 10 more working, participating people in our community and 10 fewer prisoners in our jails. At an average yearly cost of approximately $25,000 to house an inmate in this state, not only will we save the $250,000 per year it would cost to keep them locked up, we'll have the added benefit of them paying into a system they would otherwise be taking from.

More important may be what it will mean to those who make new lives for themselves outside the criminal justice system. They will no longer regard crime and imprisonment as an acceptable way of life. Their futures will hold promise and hopefulness as they realize the empowerment that comes with education. Frustration and the fear of being punished will be replaced with confidence and faith in a system that will reward them for their accomplishments. Their children will grow up in homes where education is valued and won't have to experience the desperation that comes from a life of crime. For those who change their behavior through education and other community support programs the cycles of illiteracy and adversity will be broken.

The GED classes are only one part of a comprehensive education program that, through collaborations with Central Piedmont Community College, Charlotte-Mecklenburg Schools and other community service agencies, provides classes and workshops to the inmates at the jail. Included are English as a Second Language, substance abuse, domestic violence and life skills classes.

The small investment we make in the lives of the people who benefit from these programs today will produce dividends in the future that are impossible to calculate.

PART 2

■ DISCUSSION QUESTIONS

1. What factors, both internal and external, do you think are important in the development of aggressive and delinquent behaviors?
2. Recidivism rates are very high in juvenile delinquents. What factors do you feel play important roles in the stability of these behaviors over time?
3. The article suggests that education can reduce recidivism rates for juvenile offenders. What factors do you think account for this finding?
4. Can you think of other rehabilitation options that may be successful in reducing recidivism rates? How might these other options positively affect juvenile offenders?
5. Some people would argue that prevention is more effective than rehabilitation. Discuss how you might prevent a child from becoming a criminal. At what age should the prevention be aimed and what particular aspect of the child's functioning should be targeted?

■ SUGGESTED READINGS

Elliot, D. S. (1994). Serious violent offenders: Onset, developmental course, and termination. The American Society of Criminology 1993 Presidential Address. *Criminology, 32,* 1–21.

Loeber, R. & Dishion, T. J. (1983). Early predictors of male delinquency: A review. *Psychological Bulletin, 94,* 68–99.

Offord, D. R., Boyle, M. H., & Racine, Y. A. (1991). The epidemiology of antisocial behavior in childhood and adolescence. In Pepler, D. J.,

Rubin, K. H. (Eds.), *The development and treatment of childhood aggression* (pp. 31–54). Hillsdale, NJ, Lawrence Erlbaum, 1991.

Skogan, W. G. (1989). Social change and the future of violent crime. In T. R. Gurr (Ed.), *Violence in America: Vol. 1, The history of crime.* Newbury Park, CA: Sage.

Snyder, H., & Sickmund, M. (1999). *Juvenile offenders and victims: 1999 National Report,* p. 63. Washington, DC: Office of Juvenile Justice and Delinquency Prevention.

Berke, R. L. (1994, January 23). *Crime joins economic issues as leading worry, poll says. New York Times.*

Huesmann, L. R., & Miller, L. S. (1994). Long-term effects of repeated exposure to media violence in childhood. In L. R. Huesmann (Ed.), *Aggressive behavior: Current perspectives* (pp. 153–186). New York: Plenum Press.

MODULE 24

BREUER AND THE CASE OF ANNA O.

In this module, you will have a chance to apply your understanding of Psychoanalytic theory to an original case study treated by Josef Breuer a contemporary and protégée of Sigmund Freud, the originator of psychoanalysis. For this exercise, you will read the case study of Anna O and answer the following questions meant to facilitate discussion.

INTRODUCTION

Breuer was a Viennese physician and protégée of Sigmund Freud in the 19th century. Anna O was under the care of Breuer, although Freud later used this case to illustrate his theory of psychoanalysis and to develop the treatment of the "talking cure."

Among the innovations of psychoanalytic theory was an emphasis on how events in childhood may affect the development of mental disorder later in the life course. As such, psychoanalysis was one of the first theories of abnormal psychology to recognize the importance of developmental themes.

Other classic cases, such as that of Little Hans, present more vivid depictions of Freud's stages of sexual development and the implication of unresolved stage-salient conflicts for later disorder. However, the case of Anna O presents a young woman who is just entering adulthood and presents with an illness referred to at the time as hysteria. Although we would describe her symptoms differently today, hysteria was a well-recognized disorder in 19th century Europe.

For Part 1 of this module, we have reprinted an abstract describing the case of Anna O as presented by Spitzer, Skodol, Gibbon and Williams (1983). For Part 2, we have posed questions about psychoanalytic theory and this case.

PART 1
REQUIRED READING

ANNA O

From Psychopathology: A Case Book *by R. Spitzer. Copyright © 1983 by McGraw-Hill Companies Inc. Reprinted by permission of McGraw-Hill Companies, Inc.*

Anna O was the only daughter of a wealthy Viennese Jewish family. She became ill when she was 21, in 1880.

> "Up to the onset of the disease, the patient showed no sign of nervousness, not even during pubescence. She had a keen, intuitive intellect, a craving for psychic fodder, which she did not, however, receive after she left school. She was endowed with a sensitiveness for poetry and fantasy, which was, however, controlled by a very strong and critical mind ... Her will was energetic, impenetrable and persevering, sometimes mounting to selfishness; it relinquished its aim only out of kindness and for the sake of others ... Her moods always showed a slight tendency to an excess of merriment or sadness, which made her more or less temperamental ... With her puritanically minded family, this girl of overflowing mental vitality led a most monotonous existence."

She spent hours daydreaming, making up fanciful plots in what she called her "private theater." She was at times so engrossed in fantasy that she did not hear when people spoke to her.

In July, 1880, her father, whom she admired and "loved passionately," developed tuberculosis. From July through November Anna was his night nurse, sitting up with him every night observing his pain and deterioration, with the knowledge that he would not recover.

Her own health eventually began to decline:

> "... she became very weak, anemic, and evinced a disgust for nourishment, so that despite her marked reluctance, it was found necessary to take her away from the sick man. The main reason for this step was a very intensive cough about which I [Breuer] was first consulted. I found that she had a typical nervous cough. Soon, there also developed a striking need for rest, distinctly noticeable in the afternoon hours, which merged in the evening into a sleeplike state, followed by strong excitement ... From the eleventh of December until the first of April the patient remained bedridden.

> "In rapid succession there seemingly developed a series of new and severe disturbances.

> "Left-sided occipital pain; convergent strabismus (diplopia), which was markedly aggravated through excitement. She complained that the wall was falling over (obliquous affection). Profound analyzable visual disturbances, paresis of the anterior muscles of the throat, to the extent that the head could finally be moved only if the patient pressed it backward between her raised shoulders and then moved her whole back. Contractures and anesthesia of the right upper extremity, and somewhat later of the right lower extremity ...

> "It was in this condition that I took the patient under treatment, and I soon became convinced that we were confronted with a severe psychic alteration. There were two entirely separate states of consciousness, which alternated very frequently and spontaneously, moving further apart during the course of the disease. In one of them she knew her environment, was sad and anxious, but relatively normal; in the other, she hallucinated, was 'naughty'—i.e., she scolded, threw the pillows at people whenever and to what extent her contractures enabled her to, and tore with her movable fingers the buttons from the covers and underwear, etc. If anything had been changed in the room during this phrase, if someone entered, or went out, she then complained that she was lacking in time, and observed the gap in the lapse of her conscious ideas ... In very clear moments she com-

plained of the deep darkness in her head, that she could not think, that she was going blind and deaf, and that she had two egos, her real and an evil one, which forced her to evil things, etc. . . . there appeared a deep, functional disorganization of her speech. At first, it was noticed that she missed words; gradually, when this increased her language was devoid of all grammar, all syntax, to the extent that the whole conjugation of verbs was wrong . . . In the further course of this development she missed words almost continuously, and searched for them laboriously in four or five languages, so that one could hardly understand her . . . She spoke only English and understood nothing that was told her in German. The people about her were forced to speak English . . . There then followed two weeks of complete mutism. Continuous effort to speak elicited no sound.

"About ten days after her father died, a consultant was called in whom she ignored as completely as all strangers, while I demonstrated to him her peculiarities . . . It was a real 'negative hallucination,' which has so often been reproduced experimentally since then. He finally succeeded in attracting her attention by blowing smoke into her face. She then suddenly saw a stranger, rushed to the door, grabbed the key, but fell to the floor unconscious. This was followed by a short outburst of anger, and then by a severe attack of anxiety, which I could calm only with a great deal of effort."

The family was afraid she would jump from the window, so she was removed from her third-floor apartment to a country house where, for three days

> ". . . she remained sleepless, too, no nourishment, and was full of suicidal ideas . . . She also broke windows, etc., and evinced hallucinations [of black snakes, death's heads, etc.] without absences [dissociated periods.]

Breuer treated her by asking her, under hypnosis, to talk about her symptoms, a technique which she referred to as "chimney sweeping." As the treatment proceeded, she had longer periods of lucidity and began to lose her symptoms. After eighteen months of treatment, as Anna prepared to spend the summer in her country home, Breuer pronounced her well and said he would no longer be seeing her. That evening he was called back to the house, where he found Anna thrashing around in her bed, going through an imaginary childbirth. She insisted that the baby was Breuer's. He managed to calm her by hypnotizing her. According to Ernest Jones, Breuer then "fled the house in a cold sweat" and never saw her again.

Anna remained ill intermittently over the next six years, spending considerable time in a sanatorium, where she apparently became addicted to morphine. She was often fairly well in the daytime, but still suffered from hallucinatory states toward evening.

By 30 she had apparently completely recovered, and moved to Franton with her mother. There she became a feminist leader and social worker. She established an institution for "wayward girls" and spoke out against the devaluation of women which she believed was inherent in Orthodox Judaism.

She never married, but was said to be an attractive and passionate woman who gathered admirers wherever she went. She had no recurrences of her illness and never spoke about them—in fact, she apparently asked her relatives not to speak of it to anyone. In her later years the attitude toward psychoanalysis was clearly negative, and she became quite angry at the suggestion that one of her "girls" be psychoanalyzed.

Anna died at 77, of abdominal cancer.

PART 2
Discussion Questions

1. Can you identify what Breuer might have considered symptoms of Anna O's mental illness?

2. Find in the description of Anna O's case, examples of Freud's concepts of ego defense mechanisms, fixation and regression and unconscious repression of desires.
3. How does Freud's theory of psychosexual stages affect Breuer's interpretation of Anna O's case?
4. Pick one of the salient symptoms exhibited by Anna O and use Psychoanalytic theory to describe specific mechanisms by which such symptoms might have been formed.
5. How might the identification of these behaviors as symptoms be related to the 19th century European society in which Breuer and Freud lived and worked? How do you think Anna O would be viewed in today's world.
6. The case of Anna O does not necessarily present a successful psychoanalytic intervention. What do you think went wrong in this treatment? Why would you think that she might have improved as she got older?
7. What unique aspects of Anna O's developmental history might have played a role in the onset of her illness as well as her recovery?

■ Suggested Readings

The Case Study of Anna O is but one of the original case studies first published in 1895 by Breuer and Freud in *Studies in Hysteria* (translated by Brill in 1937). For a full account of this case, please refer to Breuer and Freud, *Studies in Hysteria,* translated by Brill. Beacon Press, Boston, 1937, p. 14.

MODULE 25

AUTISM AND MINDBLINDNESS

In this module, you will learn more about autism, a pervasive developmental disorder that is characterized by impairments in verbal and nonverbal communication, deficits in social cognition, and an insistence on repetition and routine. An article on this topic is included along with discussion questions.

■ INTRODUCTION

It is estimated that about 1 in 500 children will be diagnosed with autism, although the prevalence rate has been increasing recently with greater awareness of the disorder and its symptoms. There is currently no consistent physiological or neurological profile for autism, meaning that diagnoses are made primarily based on behavioral symptoms. In order to clarify this profile, research has been accumulated over the past few decades that attempts to describe the cognitive and social characteristics of autism. Interestingly, there is still considerable debate concerning the primary impairment of the autistic mind. One of the most recent and influential theories to emerge on this topic contends that individuals with autism are characterized by *mindblindness*, a deficit in the ability to consider the feelings, thoughts, or points of view of other people.

The article that follows from *Newsweek* magazine describes in greater detail both mindblindness and autism more generally. Following the article, a series of questions are presented in order to elicit a discussion on the subject.

PART 1
■ REQUIRED READING

UNDERSTANDING AUTISM

More kids than ever are facing the challenge of *mindblindness*. The causes are still a mystery, but research is offering new clues to how the brain works.

Geoffrey Cowley
NEWSWEEK

From Newsweek, *July 31, 2000,* © *2000 Newsweek, Inc. All rights reserved. Reprinted by permission.*

He took up screaming instead of sleeping at night, and almost any sensory stimulation, even the touch of clothing against his skin, seemed to upset him. Russell's mother, Janna, remembers carrying him upstairs for a bath one night when he was 20 months old. When she called him her baby boy, he said, "I not a baby—I a big boy!" It was the last full sentence he ever spoke.

In the years since, Janna and her husband, Rik, have tried everything short of witchcraft to get their child back. Russell follows a special diet and takes dozens of supplements each day. He's had speech therapy and behavioral therapy and made his way into special-ed classes at a local elementary school. His parents are thrilled by his progress—"Any little improvement is a victory," Janna says. But drop in as Russell gets home from school, and you see what the family is up against. Pushing the door open, he flaps his arms and makes a guttural sound before accepting a hug from each parent. He doesn't seem to notice the stranger in the room until his mom urges him to say hello. He honors the request, yet his clear blue eyes reveal no hint of engagement. "He tests in the normal range for intelligence," his dad says. "But he can't tell me how his day was, or what hurts."

People like Russell are not as rare as you'd think. Autism stalks every sector of society, and its recognized incidence is exploding. In California, the number of receiving state services for autistic disorders has nearly quadrupled since 1987, rising 15 percent in the past three months alone. Nationally, the demand for such services rose by 556 percent during the '90s. Some experts see a growing epidemic in these numbers, while others believe they reflect new awareness of an existing problem. Either way, autism is now thought to affect one person in 500, making it more common than Down syndrome or childhood cancer. "This is not a rare disorder," says Dr. Marie Bristol Power of the National Institute of Child Health and Human Development (NICHD). "It's a pressing public-health problem."

And a profound mystery. Nearly six decades after autism was first formally recognized, the big questions—What causes it? Can it be prevented or cured?—are still wide open. But the pace of discovery is accelerating. Scientists are gaining tantalizing insights into the autistic mind, with its odd capacity for genius as well as detachment. And though the suspected causes range from genetic mutations to viruses and toxic chemicals, we now know it's a brain-based developmental disorder and not a result of poor parenting (accepted wisdom as recently as the 1970s). The condition may never be eradicated, but science is making autistic life more livable, and enriching our whole understanding of the mind.

Until fairly recently, neuroscientists thought of autism as a single, utterly debilitating condition. Like Russell, people with the classic form of the condition lack normal language ability, and they seem devoid of social impulses. A classically autistic child may tug on someone's arm to get a need met, but he (four out of five sufferers are male) won't spontaneously play peekaboo or share his delight in a toy. Nor will he engage in pretend play, using a banana, say, as a pistol or a telephone. What he will do is fixate on a pet interest—doorknobs, for instance, or license plates—and resist any change in routine. A new route to the grocery store can spark a major tantrum. Three out of four classically autistic people are thought to be mentally retarded. A third suffer from epilepsy, and most end up in institutions by the age of 13. "It's like 'The Village of the Damned'," says Portia Iverson, cofounder of the activist group Cure Autism Now and mother of an autistic 8-year-old named Dov. "It's as if someone has stolen into your house during the night and left your child's bewildered body behind."

As it turns out, though, autism has more than one face. During the 1940s, a Viennese pediatrician named Hans Asperger described a series of young patients who were somewhat autistic but still capable of functioning at a fairly high level.

These "little professors" had quick tongues and sharp minds. They might stand too close and speak in loud monotones, but they could hold forth eloquently on their pet interests. Asperger's work went unread in the English-speaking world for several decades, but its rediscovery in the early

> **ADVICE FOR PARENTS**
>
> **AUTISM IS A LIFELONG CONDITION,**
> **BUT EARLY ACTION CAN MAKE IT LESS DEVASTATING**
>
> - Get a diagnosis. If you're concerned, see a doctor who's familiar with autism. Don't assume the child will catch up.
> - Get help. Special schooling and speech therapy are often critical.
> - Know your rights. The government mandates services. Consult the National Information Center for Children and Youth With Disabilities (nichcy.org/index.html).
> - Seek support. Resources include the National Alliance for Autism Research (naar.org), the Autism Society of America (autism-society.org), Autism Resources (autism-info.com) and Families for the Early Treatment of Autism (feat.org).

1980s started a revolution that is still unfolding. Experts now use terms like "Asperger disorder" and "pervasive development disorder" to describe mild variants of autism. And as the umbrella expands, more and more people are coming under it.

What, ultimately, makes autistic people different? How do they experience the world? Twenty years ago no one had much of a clue. But a burgeoning body of research now suggests that the core of all autism is a syndrome known as mindblindness. For most of us, mind reading comes as naturally as walking or chewing. We readily deduce what other people know and what they don't, and we understand implicitly that thoughts and feelings are revealed in gestures, facial expressions and tone of voice. An autistic person may sense none of this. In one of the first studies to highlight this issue, researchers quizzed children about a scenario in which a girl named Sally places a marble in a covered basket and leaves the room. While Sally is out, her friend Anne moves the marble from the basket into a nearby covered box. When asked where Sally would later look for her marble, even retarded children knew she would expect to find it where she'd left it. By contrast, most autistic children thought she would look in the box. They couldn't see the world through Sally's eyes.

Autistic people can master Sally-Anne scenarios with practice, but subtler mind-reading tasks still stump them. They fail tests of "second-order belief attribution." (If Sally watches John get a miscue about an object's location, where will she expect him to look for it?) And even the most brilliant Asperger sufferers are easily flummoxed by facial expressions. In one recent study, Cambridge University psychologist Simon Baron-Cohen asked three of them—a physicist, a computer scientist and a mathematician—to match pictures of people's eyes to words like "grateful" or "preoccupied." They were lost. The clear implication is that our brains are wired for certain kinds of social awareness—and that this circuitry can fail even as the rest of the organ thrives.

It's not hard to see how mindblindness would derail a person's social development. If you can't perceive mental states, you can't show empathy, practice deceit or distinguish a joke from a threat—let alone make friends. Sharing becomes pointless when you can't see its effects on people, and conversation loses much of its meaning because you miss the unspoken intentions that hold it together.

Ten-year-old Jace Covert of Sagaponack, N.Y., is always falling into that trap. When an adult friend buys him a cookie, saying it "has your name all over it," he replies earnestly that he can't see it there. Jace is not autistic in the way that Russell Rollens is. Jace spent several years in a mainstream private school and kept up with the curriculum. But his social ineptitude made him a magnet for ridicule. Lacking the tools to deflect it, he resorted to hitting, and the school eased him out. Jace is now thriving in public school with the help of a social-skills program, but his prospects are hard to gauge. "Will my son ever know what it feels like to fall in love?" his mother asks. "What kind of work will be available to him? Those are the questions I ask myself."

Romance is predictably difficult for autistic people, but many do brilliantly in certain lines of work. Only rarely does an autistic savant come along who can memorize a book in 10 minutes or measure the exact height of a building by glancing at it. But one autistic person in 10 shows exceptional skill in areas such as art, music, calculation or memory. And because they share a cognitive style known as "weak central coherence," they consistently excel on certain mental tasks. Whereas most of us use context and categories to sort our perceptions, people with autism tend to view the world as an array of discrete particulars. "My concept of ships is linked to every specific one I've ever known," says Temple Grandin, the autistic author and livestock scientist. "There is a Queen Mary and a Titanic, but there is no generic 'ship.'"

Sometimes that's just as well. As the British psychologists Uta Frith and Francesca Happe have shown recently, autistic people's blindness to contextual cues helps them resist optical illusions. People with autism also have a strong advantage on "embedded figures" tests, which involve finding a simple shape hidden in a complex design (graphic). And they're masters at telling similar objects apart. With prolonged exposure, anyone starts noticing the uniqueness of things that look identical at a glance; that's why experienced bird watchers are so good at spotting different subspecies of warblers. People with autism don't experience this effect. Where others see forests, they see trees from the start.

People can build lives around these talents. Thirty-one-year-old Eric Spencer of Flemington, N.J., started reading when he was 18 months old. His autism has always confined him to well-controlled environments; he lives near his parents, aided by a "life-skills coordinator." But his love of letters—individual letters—has been a lifeline. A local library has exhibited his calligraphy, and he sometimes visits nursery schools to carve children's names from poster board for them. To earn money, he sorts documents at Ortho-MacNeil Pharmaceuticals. "My job," he says, "is getting along perfectly."

How do people end up this way? Why do their minds exhibit these quirks? "We're at a very primitive stage of research," says David Amaral, a neuroscientist at the University of California, Davis, and research director at the MIND Institute, which just received $34 million in state funding to study autism and other neurological disorders. "We don't know what causes autism, or which areas of the brain are most affected." Autopsies of autistic people have found that cells in the "limbic" regions that mediate social behavior are often small and densely packed, suggesting their early development was interrupted. And neural-imaging studies are showing differences in how autistic and nonautistic brains respond to social cues, such as faces or eyes. Researchers at Stanford are now launching a multicenter study to identify the most salient ones and assess their significance.

Other scientists are zeroing in on possible differences in brain chemistry. This spring, in a preliminary study, a team led by Dr. Karin Nelson of the National Institutes of Health discovered what may be a chemical marker for autism. The researchers identified 246 teenagers whose blood had been sampled at birth as part of the California Newborn Screening Program. Some of the teens were healthy, while others suffered from autism, cerebral palsy or mental retardation. And when the scientists examined their early blood samples, those from the autistic or retarded kids showed high levels of four proteins involved in brain development (VIP, CGRP, BDNF and NT4). The findings "suggest that some abnormal process is already underway at birth," says Dr. Judith Grether, a California epidemiologist who coauthored the study. If further research confirms the pattern, we may someday be able to test prenatally for autism.

Unfortunately, we still won't know what precipitates the condition. There is no question that heredity leaves some people susceptible. Roughly 5 percent of kids with autistic siblings have autistic disorders themselves (that's about 25 times the usual rate). And the risk of autism is 75 percent (375 times higher than usual) among people with affected identical twins. Researchers are studying "hot spots" on several chromosomes that could harbor culpable genes, but none of those regions has been linked consistently to the disorder. Experts assume the problem stems not from a single gene but from 10 or more that occur in combinations. "Everyone agrees there is a genetic predisposition," says Bristol Power of the NICHD. "The question is: what triggers the condition in people who are predisposed?"

This is where things get murky. Some activists, including Rik and Janna Rollens, fear that childhood vaccines may trigger autistic disorders in susceptible kids. Others suspect that toxic substances are somehow to blame. Bobbie and Billy Gallagher started to wonder about environmental hazards several years ago, after two of their three kids were diagnosed as autistic. The Gallaghers live in Brick Township, N.J., a working-class town with a well-known toxic landfill. And when they sought out other afflicted kids, they were surprised to find 44 of them among Brick's 71,000 residents. Two years ago they demanded an inquiry, and they got one. In a report released this spring, federal investigators concluded that Brick's rate of autistic disorders was three times the 1 in 500 usually cited as the norm. They noted that small, intensive studies often find rates this high—an indication that the official estimates may be low—

but they found nothing in the landfill, the water supply or the local river that looked like a plausible culprit.

That isn't to say toxic substances are off the hook. Many of the babies exposed prenatally to thalidomide during the late '50s suffered from autism as well as defects, and other substances could turn out to have similar effects. Dr. Eric Hollander of New York's Mount Sinai School of Medicine noticed several years ago that 60 percent of the autistic patients in his clinic had been exposed in the womb to pitocin, the synthetic version of a brain chemical (oxytocin) that helps induce labor. That could be significant, since only 20 percent of all births are assisted by pitocin. Or it could be a meaningless coincidence. In the hope of finding out, Hollander is now tracking 58,000 kids whose mothers' treatments were monitored during pregnancy.

Until we know how to prevent autistic disorders, the challenge will be to help people compensate for them. The parents of autistic kids often swear by unconventional remedies (secretin, facilitated communication, auditory integration, special diets), but the benefits are unproven at best. Tranquilizers and antidepressants can help ease the anxiety and compulsiveness that autism causes, and stimulants such as Ritalin can help affected kids shift their attention more easily. But no medication can correct the disorder itself, and none is likely to take the place of intensive schooling.

The standard approach, known as Applied Behavioral Analysis (ABA), involves conditioning kids through constant reinforcement to behave appropriately. That's the technique at Sacramento's ABC School, a day school that boasts four teachers to every five kids. Whatever the task at hand—using words, recognizing facial expressions—the teachers break it into discrete units and drill the kids repeatedly. Every success earns a token, and six tokens earn a cookie. To help nonverbal kids communicate, teachers give them notebooks filled with icons. When 4-year-old Chris hands teacher Jessica the icon for cheese, she gives him a piece and says, "I want cheese," linking the phrase with the reward. Over time, 70 percent of the kids using this Picture Exchange Communication System (PECS) learn to make simple utterances.

These routines are a godsend for kids like Kyle and Ian Brown of Long Beach, Calif. The 8-year-old twins have never been easy. They climb furniture, leap from stairways and scale six-foot fences. Ian once made his way onto the nearby freeway. Lauren, their 9-year-old sister, displays only fondness as Kyle slaps his cheek rhythmically and Ian circles the kitchen table, clicking his tongue as he tries to snatch a can of soda. "But it's hard here," she says. "Everything's locked—even my room." Late last year the twins' parents thought they'd have to place them in an institution. But when an ABA-oriented school opened in Huntington Beach, they signed the boys up. Six months later both are starting to brush their teeth and dress themselves, and Kyle is saying things like "I want to go for a walk" instead of banging his head in frustration. Ian's language is limited to mimicking words, but he uses PECS to express needs. Dinners out are still unthinkable. But now, so is sending them away.

The ABA approach isn't right for everyone. Educators can often help higher-functioning kids build on their own skills and interests. Six-year-old Jack Guild of Greenwich, Conn., can be hard to reach, even though he has no trouble with language. "As a baby he was not loving or responsive," his mother, Cathy, recalls. "And as he got older the tantrums got worse. Every transition—bed to breakfast, home to school—was a flash point." When Jack started seeing caseworkers at the Greenwich Autism Program last year, they didn't drill him on getting dressed. They helped Cathy devise routines that would heighten his sense of control—simple things like letting him finish a favorite video in the morning, then driving him to school instead of coaxing him to walk. The results have been dramatic. "I feel like I have my kid back," she says. "A kid who can learn and develop."

As different as they sound, both strategies rest on an understanding that autistic kids are not willfully misbehaving, just trying to navigate a world they're not equipped to fathom. As Dr. Fred Volkmar of Yale wrote recently, the worst possible fate for such a child is to be placed in a program for troublemakers. When that happens, he says, "a perfect victim" is surrounded by "perfect victimizers." If the new autism awareness accomplishes nothing else, it should spare many children that fate. With luck, it will also get them recognized early, when special interventions can still help. Only 10 percent of the autistic children entering the celebrated Princeton Child Development

Center after age 5 go on to enter mainstream schools—yet half of those recognized earlier end up making the transition. Until autism can be prevented or cured, that's a goal to strive for.

With Donna Foote in Los Angeles and Heather Won Tesoriero in New York

PART 2
Discussion Questions

1. Imagine that you are a person with high functioning autism or Asperger syndrome. How would you experience the world differently than you do now? If you were asked what it is like to be autistic, what would you say?
2. What is meant by mindblindness? How does this concept further our understanding of the autistic mind?
3. The article details some of the difficulties children with high-functioning autism have making friends, understanding social conventions, and fitting in with their peers. What suggestions would you make to educators in order to optimize such a child's experiences in school?
4. After reading various characteristics of individuals with autism, how would you suggest that environments be structured in order to maximize their strengths and minimize their weaknesses? Can you think of potential career paths that may cater to the strengths of a person with high-functioning autism?
5. There are a few researchers who feel that high-functioning autism/Asperger syndrome is more of a cognitive style than a disorder. Based on your reading of the article, would you agree? Why or why not?
6. There is currently no cure for autism. According to the article, which interventions offer the best prognosis for individuals with autism? If you were the parent of a child with autism, what types of treatment would you seek? How would you handle the challenge of raising a child with autism?

Suggested Readings

Baron-Cohen, S. (1995). *Mindblindness: An essay on autism and theory of mind*. MIT Press, Cambridge, MA.

Grandin, T. (1995). *Thinking in pictures, and other reports from my life with autism*. Vintage, New York.

Sacks, O. (1993). An anthropologist on mars, *The New Yorker*. December 27, pp. 106–125.

MODULE 26

RISK AND PROTECTIVE FACTORS IN DEVELOPMENT: A FILM ANALYSIS

In this module you will think about child and adolescent psychopathology from a developmental perspective. In this multi-part assignment you will first read an article on the classification of child psychopathology (Garber, 1984). You will then watch a movie (such as *Marvin's Room*, *What's Eating Gilbert Grape*, or *Hoop Dreams*). Finally, you will answer a series of questions in preparation for class discussion.

INTRODUCTION

A variety of systems for classifying psychopathology in children and adolescents has been proposed and debated in the literature. In this module you will read about and utilize one set of criteria (Garber, 1984), designed to examine these issues from a developmental perspective. Instead of relying solely on the use of adult criteria or on the diagnosis of a childhood disorder at one point in time, you will consider childhood psychopathology in terms of patterns of behavior that exist within environmental contexts. In thinking about this topic, keep in mind Garber's question of normality and deviance with respect to age, context, and the progression of development over time. In addition to classifying a movie character, you will be asked to reflect on the possible existence of the character's resiliency, on how he or she responded to stress or adversity, and on what potential risk and protective factors were at work in his or her context.

PART 1
REQUIRED READING

Garber, J. (1984). Classification and childhood psychopathology: A developmental perspective. *Child Development, 55,* 30–48.

Note: For this assignment it is sufficient to read pages 30–44.

PART 2
WATCH A MOVIE

Suggestion: *Marvin's Room*, *What's Eating Gilbert Grape*, or *Hoop Dreams*.

PART 3
DISCUSSION QUESTIONS

1. Describe the problem depicted in the film. Who was the identified patient or client in the movie? What was the nature of the problem?
2. How might you have seen the problem change over time?
3. What evidence for the problem was provided in the movie? (If there is more than one identified patient, choose one to focus on in this analysis.) Note that you may not think that there are any problems that are significant enough to meet criteria for psychopathology. However, we are assuming that someone has brought this client into your office. Pick the issue that seems to be the most pressing.
4. Evaluate the problem against Garber's criteria for determining whether psychopathology is present. The film may not present enough data at times to provide a clear evaluation of these criteria. If the data is not present, say so, and clarify what else you would want to know to determine whether the identified client would meet these criteria. If the client's history does not meet criteria, then demonstrate why it does not.
5. What risk factors do you think contributed to the development of the problem that you described. How might these risk factors have interacted with the age, gender or other contextual factors of the identified client to produce the manifested problems that you describe? Give examples of these factors.
6. Indicate what protective factors you think might have lessened the severity of the problem you observed in the identified client. Are there other factors that you think could have reduced the client's risk for disorder or problematic outcomes if they had been present?
7. What prognosis would you give the identified client? Are there significant factors that could change the course of the disorder (and change your mind about the prognosis)? If so, what might some of those factors be?

SUGGESTED READINGS

Marsh, E. J. & Wolfe, D. A. (Eds) (2002). *Abnormal child psychology*, Second Edition, (Chapters 1 and 2). Belmont, CA: Wadsworth.

Rutter, M. (1987). Psychosocial resilience and protective mechanisms. *American Journal of Orthopsychiatry, 57,* 316–331.

Rutter, M. & Sroufe, L. A. (2000). Development and psychopathology: Concepts and challenges. *Development and Psychopathology, 12,* 265–296.